DENTAL OFFICE RESCUE

ZEROED-IN SOLUTIONS FOR WINNING PATIENTS WHO STAY, PAY, AND REFER

LINDA KANE

Linda Kane -- 1st ed.
Chief Editor, Shannon Buritz
ISBN: 978-1-954757-45-5

The Publisher has strived to be as accurate and complete as possible in the creation of this book.

This book is not intended for use as a legal, business, accounting, or financial advice source. All readers are advised to seek the services of competent professionals in legal, business, accounting, and finance fields.

Like anything else in life, there are no guarantees of income or results in practical advice books. Readers are cautioned to rely on their judgment about their individual circumstances to act accordingly.

While all attempts have been made to verify information provided in this publication, the Publisher assumes no responsibility for errors, omissions, or contrary interpretation of the subject matter herein. Any perceived slights of specific persons, peoples, or organizations are unintentional.

This book is dedicated to Parker, my amazing son, who always supports me; to my beautiful fur babies, Piper and Koko, who give unconditional love; and to my parents and family for their continuing love and support of my big dream! I am what I am today because of you!

CONTENTS

INTRODUCTION

In my experience working closely with dental practices, I've discovered a universal wish among dentists—a wish for a steady stream of new patients who return for ongoing care, embrace recommended treatment, and settle their bills without delay. The vision is clear: a dental office bustling with satisfied patients, unwavering loyalty, and commitment to their oral health supported by their trust in their dental care provider. This dream illustrates the essence of a thriving practice, as new patients are the lifeblood that sustains and propels a practice forward.

A drama-free, cohesive team is an equally important component of the ideal dental practice scenario. The environment would be free from internal conflicts, where each team member feels valued, understood, and integrated into the overall mission of the practice. A cohesive team enhances patient experience, improves workflow efficiency, and contributes to a positive workplace culture, attracting and retaining patients and staff.

Many dental practices operate within an "invisible box," adhering to routines and methodologies that have seemingly worked for years. This comfort zone, characterized by a consistent income and a stable team, often blinds practitioners to the evolving needs of their practice and the potential for improvement. The biggest issue is lack of training or lack of awareness that training even exists. This gap in knowledge and skills, especially in non-clinical areas such as patient communication and front desk operations, significantly decreases a practice's ability to reach its full potential and maximize its revenue cycle.

Communication, empathy, and customer service—skills critical to the success of any dental office—are often overlooked. A front desk that lacks warmth or has a dismissive tone can inadvertently turn patients away. The intricacies of managing a dental practice, particularly the front office, which I call the "cockpit" or "brains of the operation," remain a mystery to many dentists. Their training focuses on clinical excellence inside a mouth, leaving a void when managing the business aspects of their practice. This undertraining of front desk staff can lead to unintentional consequences, such as fraud or embezzlement, and it's not their fault. At the end of the day, each staff member is doing the best they can with the tools they have.

Beyond the operational challenges lies a deeper, more personal fear among dentists—the fear of failure. Despite its noble intentions and significant impact on public health, the dental profession carries a heavy emotional toll. In the United States, dentistry ranks as the second profession most associated with suicide, a sad indicator of the pressures and fears dentists face daily.

These fears encompass a wide range of concerns, from the dread of legal battles and the inability to meet financial obligations to the challenges of retaining and compensating a talented team during an employment crisis. The pressure to maintain a particular lifestyle immediately after graduation further exacerbates the situation, plunging young dentists into a "mountain of debt."

The combination of high expectations, intense work, and financial burdens can lead to overwhelming stress and, in some cases, depression. This book aims to offer practical advice for improving the operational efficiency of dental practices that will, in turn, support dentists' emotional and psychological well-being. By confronting these challenges head-on, we can pave the way for a more fulfilling, successful, and healthy professional life for dentists and their teams.

Contributing to these fears is the apprehension over insurance. Every dentist hates dealing with insurance, but they also know that these partnerships are necessary for attracting new patients and ensuring the financial accessibility of dental care. The feeling of being "held over a barrel" by insurance requirements is a significant source of skepticism and discomfort. However, as discussed in the following chapters, there is a smart, strategic way to foster beneficial relationships with insurance companies to expand your patient base without feeling compromised or undervalued.

We will also tackle other questions and concerns that may keep you up at night, including…

- *"How do I establish the systems in my office to grow the practice?"*
- *"How do I hire a team that will be loyal and supportive of our practice goals?"*
- *"I know nothing about the front desk - is help even available?"*

Each concern highlights a key area of practice management that, when effectively addressed, can significantly impact overall performance and staff and patient satisfaction.

Envisioning Success: Beyond the Practice

Dentists receiving good counsel are not focusing on the "right now" but rather on what they want the end of their careers to look like. It's about envisioning the end goal, the legacy you wish to leave behind, and crafting a career aligning with this vision.

"You basically get 16 summers with your kids," I often remind my clients, which stresses the importance of prioritizing time with family and structuring practice hours to support this priority. This approach embodies the principle of "if you build it, they will come," suggesting that by setting firm boundaries around work hours, you can still attract the clientele necessary for a thriving practice. The "secret sauce" for a fulfilling career in dentistry involves making decisions with a clear plan—prioritizing time with family, avoiding unnecessary debt, and making smart investments in the practice.

How do I know? The truth is, I've been doing this for a very long time. Unlike other "consultants," I've been in the dental industry for over 25 years and in the weeds like you. I've stepped into nearly bankrupt offices and helped them transform into $3 million practices in one year. Implementing my private practice principles has brought the lowest-ranking corporate offices to top-tier practices. I have the steps, tools, resources, and network to make a difference. Simply stated, I'm just passionate about helping private practice dental offices thrive!

My commitment focuses on uplifting the often overlooked and unheard front office teams. These teams are the unsung heroes of dental practices, tirelessly working without due recognition or awareness that help is available. This book is a guide for those ready to look beyond the immediate and embrace the possibilities of what their practice could become. It is an invitation to zero in on success, not just in financial terms but as a balance between professional achievement and personal fulfillment. Let's get started.

- Linda Kane

PART ONE

FRONTLINE SUCCESS

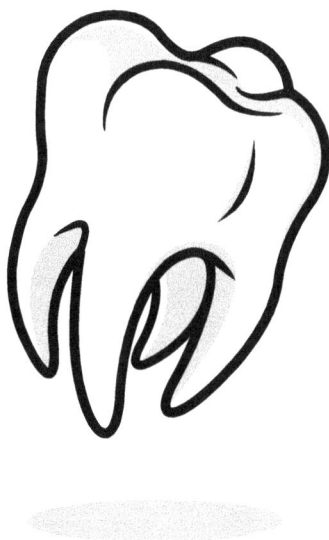

CHAPTER ONE

THE FRONT DESK:
COCKPIT OF YOUR PRACTICE

Every doctor who graduates with their degree, whether DDS or DMD, faces a significant challenge. They step into the professional world armed with clinical knowledge and skills, ready to make a difference in their patients' lives. However, a crucial piece of their education is clearly absent. They do not receive any formal education on how to run their business. This gap in their education transforms their practice into a big, scary mystery.

As I browse through social media and observe the questions experienced doctors ask and the advice they give to younger doctors—or the inquiries younger doctors pose to their more seasoned counterparts—a recurring theme emerges. They often ask, "What's the number one thing I should do with my new practice?" The unanimous advice they receive is, "Get help." Understanding that you need help because you don't know how to run your business is the first step toward success.

There's a whole complex world in the front office with tons of systems in place, and many don't realize the gravity of these systems and the impact they can have on their revenue cycle. There are roughly 26 systems in the dental practice's administrative office. This realization often comes as a surprise to many who might think it's all about answering the phone and making appointments. But it's so much more than that.

Each of these systems plays a pivotal role in a practice's functioning and financial health. They are interconnected, ensuring that the practice runs smoothly and efficiently. If any of these systems break down, it can have a domino effect, negatively impacting the overall revenue cycle. This chapter is your first step toward unraveling the mysteries of dental practice management.

Demystifying the Front Desk

The biggest misconception about the front desk is that anyone can fill the roles. The complexity of each one is often overlooked. Many practitioners believe transitioning duties at the front desk can be as simple as leaving a staff member sitting down with their replacement for a few days to pass on their responsibilities. But here lies the problem: there's no structured training. This oversight neglects that the front desk, the cockpit of the practice, sets the tone for the entire patient experience. The person handling the front desk is vitally important. Yet, paradoxically, it becomes the number one source of headaches for doctors and the primary stage for drama within the practice because the staff at the front desk often feel overwhelmed, watching their colleagues, like the hygienists, seemingly have an easier time, leading to disgruntlement. They don't think anyone sympathizes with the weight of their responsibilities.

The good news is there is a way to systemize the front desk to bring clarity and reduce stress. This systematic approach begins with identifying and implementing key systems first. When I work with an office, I start with an "observation and recommendation" phase. It involves observing how the team works together, how they communicate, and how tasks are handed off from the back to the front and vice versa. By understanding the dynamics of the team and their operational workflow, I can pinpoint what systems need to be put in place. Implementing these systems is more manageable than it might seem. You just have to know they exist and understand how they fit into the broader picture of practice management.

Roles and Responsibilities

The front desk is your very first point of contact, the face and voice shaping your practice's initial impression. Before a patient even sees you, the front desk greets them, sets the tone for their visit, and begins the care journey. When you diagnose a treatment, they're making it a reality by discussing it with patients, addressing concerns, and ensuring that the treatment plan is not just proposed but accepted and scheduled. They manage every financial transaction, consistently making the practice's lifeblood, revenue, flow. However, their role extends beyond just handling money; they are the frontline when patients have questions or concerns, especially when emotions run high over bills or treatments. Their ability to manage these interactions can significantly affect your practice's reputation and patient satisfaction.

They also play a part in keeping your schedule full, so that your hygienists and, by extension, you are optimally busy. Efficiency in scheduling is critical; you must create a schedule that balances revenue-generating treatments with necessary patient care. No doctor wants a day full of back-to-back fillings, so it is important to get the balance right.

Division of Tasks

Understanding the typical division of tasks at the front desk is essential for efficient operations. The structure varies depending on the size and dynamics of the practice, but let's consider an average-sized practice with one to two doctors and two to five hygienists. This setup usually requires three to four dedicated staff members to manage the front desk effectively.

- **Treatment Coordinator:** This individual focuses on maintaining the doctor's restorative schedule, verifying patient benefits, managing unscheduled treatments, and handling all case presentations. They make sure patients understand and commit to their treatment plans.
- **Hygiene & New Patient Coordinator:** Responsible for the hygiene department, this person manages the hygiene schedule, verifies patient benefits for hygiene services, and maintains an active recall program. They are often the first point of contact for new patients, setting the stage for a warm and welcoming experience.
- **Insurance Coordinator:** This role involves managing the insurance systems within the office, possibly extending to duties like payroll or accounts payable, depending on the

office's size and needs. They process and handle insurance claims, guarding against legal and financial pitfalls.

- **Office Manager/Leader:** Ideally, this person embodies the qualities of a servant leader. They are capable of performing all front desk functions while providing guidance and support to the team. They are not just overseeing operations; they're actively involved, ready to step in and assist whenever necessary.

Remember that the goal is not just to fill these positions but to empower these individuals to excel in their roles. By understanding each team member's responsibilities, you can create a supportive environment that encourages growth, fosters positive patient interactions, and drives your practice's success.

Embracing Connection

Distinguishing your practice from others doesn't necessarily stem from a place of competition but rather from the unique ability to connect and engage with patients from the moment they step into your office. The essence of setting your practice apart lies at the front desk—the very first point of contact. Having someone who's not just good with administrative tasks but also exceptional with people is crucial. We've all encountered front desk personnel who might benefit from taking a "chill pill." You want the opposite of that person: someone who is warm, engaging, and shows genuine interest in your patients.

When I train staff, I emphasize the power of engagement. Simple gestures of kindness, such as complimenting a patient's smile or engaging in light, friendly conversation, can significantly elevate the patient experience. These moments of connection make patients feel seen, understood and appreciated. The objective is cultivating a practice atmosphere characterized by kindness and unity among the team, creating an environment where patients can sense team cohesion and genuine care.

Creating a Welcoming Space

The environment also helps distinguish your practice. The waiting room should not resemble a sterile, impersonal space cluttered with advertisements and clinical reminders. Instead, it should feel like a family room —a place of comfort and warmth that eases the anxiety associated with dental visits. This approach to your waiting area design sets the tone for a positive patient experience, transitioning them from the external world into your care with comfort and reassurance.

The Pillars of Front Desk Training

In the dynamic environment of a dental practice, if there's one certainty, it's CHANGE. Whether it's due to staff turnover, personal circumstances, or the natural evolution of the practice, the need for consistent and ongoing training for the front desk team is undeniable. Retaining employees can be a constant battle, so training is necessary to build a resilient practice. It's important to prioritize these training areas:

- **Mastering the Consistency of the New Patient Experience:** The first impression sets the tone for the patient's entire relationship with your practice. Training must ensure that team members are proficient in creating a welcoming, engaging, and reassuring environment for every new patient, regardless of staff changes.

- **Effective Payment Collection:** The approach to collecting payments can significantly impact the practice's financial health. The team should be trained in conversational payment collection, using phrasing that encourages patients to think through their payment options proactively.

- **Managing Recall Programs:** A robust recall program is essential for keeping hygienist schedules full and maintaining ongoing patient care. Training should cover strategies for managing and maximizing the recall system, encouraging patients to return for necessary treatments regularly.

- **Enhancing Case Acceptance:** Every patient interaction should include clear communication about treatment plans and the importance of follow-up care. The team must be adept at ensuring every patient leaves, understands their Reason for Return (RFR), and schedules their Next Visit (NV), critical components of treatment plan acceptance and patient retention.

- **Verifying Patient Benefits:** Accurate verification of patient benefits maintains trust and transparency. The team must be trained to efficiently navigate insurance benefits, keep patient records updated, and accurately inform patients of their coverage.

- **Software Utilization:** The effective use of dental practice management software can revolutionize the front desk's efficiency and accuracy. Training should emphasize the full range of software capabilities, from patient communication to scheduling and billing, to avoid self-inflicted problems and inefficiencies.

Ongoing training and development are the keys to keeping your various systems rolling and robust. Through targeted training programs, you equip your staff with the necessary tools to excel and lay the foundation for a practice culture that values growth, learning, and excellence. This commitment to ongoing development is what ultimately distinguishes a good practice from a great one.

Turning Things Around: A Front Desk Success Story

One of the most memorable transformations I've ever participated in involved a dental practice in deep trouble and on the verge of bankruptcy. They had this huge, fancy office they had just built, but things weren't working out. Three people worked part-time at the front desk, so you never saw a consistent, familiar face upon walking in. Plus, there was someone in the back handling insurance with outdated software. You couldn't pull reliable reports out of it, and it was not user-friendly.

The first thing I did was watch. You want to observe what is really going on before jumping in and making massive changes. I looked for who was good at talking, who liked numbers, and how everyone got along. After figuring that out, I had a chat with the doctors. We needed some stability at the front, so we made a few changes in staffing to get full-time people on board. We decided who would handle what, like one person taking care of the hygiene appointments and another handling restorative appointments. A huge game changer was getting new software that worked so we could understand what was happening in the practice. I had a great relationship with a supply house at the time, and upon purchasing the software from them, they also gave the office a discount on the top 20 supplies they purchased. It was a win-win.

I spent time with each team member, showing them how to talk to patients, manage their areas, and work together better. We got the systems in place and running smoothly. We also started having fun with it, setting up a bonus program for the whole office. They could earn extra if they recommended specific treatments like fluoride or occlusal guards and met goals, which energized the entire team.

When I first got there, everyone was trying to do a bit of everything, and it was a mess. Nobody was really in charge of anything. Once we got everyone focused on specific tasks, things started to change. We worked on how to manage appointments, talk about treatments, and especially collect payments without making it awkward. Making the office a fun place to work helped a lot, too.

It took some time, but the changes we made started to show. Our collections went from less than half to between 97% and 99% of what we billed for. It was amazing to see. Everything boiled down to getting those systems in place and verifying everyone knew how to use them. Watching that office turn around from nearly closing to making $3 million in a year was something I'll never forget. This story isn't just about saving a business—it's about building a team that feels like family and an office that patients love coming back to. That's what makes the difference.

The Power of Seeking Guidance

Every dental practitioner, whether just starting or seasoned in the field, faces the same challenge—understanding the complexities of front desk operations and the business side of dentistry. Seeking help isn't a sign of weakness; it's a sign of wisdom. I've seen it time and again—those who are willing to acknowledge their limitations and seek guidance are the ones who thrive. But a word of caution: Not all guidance is created equal. Do your homework, do your research. Find a trainer who's been in the weeds, has walked the walk, and can guide you with real-world experience. Avoid the trap of endless workshops and workbooks that promise the world but deliver little in return. Choose wisely, and your practice will thank you for it.

KEY TAKEAWAYS

- ➲ Efficient front desk system management is key to a dental practice's financial health and smooth operations.

- ➲ Structured training and systematic approaches are needed for effective patient care, scheduling, and financial transactions.

- ➲ Successful practices excel in patient engagement and creating a welcoming environment from the first point of contact.

- ➲ Continuous training for front desk staff is crucial for adapting to changes and maintaining operational efficiency.

- ➲ Seeking guidance and implementing proven systems can improve financial performance, team cohesion, and patient satisfaction in struggling practices.

CHAPTER TWO
YOUR PRACTICE CULTURE

Practice culture is the intangible essence that permeates every interaction within your office, from when a patient walks in the door to completing their treatment. It sets the tone for the patient experience and can define your practice's success. Yet, it's something that's too frequently assumed rather than intentionally nurtured. As the practice owner and/or manager, it's essential to recognize that practice culture is where it all begins. Every decision and every interaction contributes to shaping the culture of your practice.

Complacency is a major threat to a positive practice culture, often creeping in unnoticed until it's too late. A practice that once thrived under a committed leader's guidance can begin to falter as new team members come and go. The principles and techniques taught in training sessions gather dust as implementation falls by the wayside. This scenario is all too common. The initial signs of complacency are subtle but telling. It starts with a lack of quality training and actual implementation. Learning is one thing, but knowledge remains stagnant without effective implementation. Signs of a healthy practice slipping become evident when schedules lighten, time for new patients dwindles, and accounts payable rise. These are the warning signs that your systems and training are slipping and complacency has taken hold.

Strategies for Overcoming Complacency

As I always say, "Systems run the practices, and people run the systems." When individuals slip back into old habits, the system starts to break down. It takes a significant mindset shift to keep things moving in the right direction.

One strategy I've found incredibly productive is holding regular team meetings. I'm a big fan of IDS (Identify, Discuss, Solve) meetings. They're a fantastic tool for identifying shortcomings in your systems. It's a time for your team to talk openly about what's working and, more importantly, what's lacking. Then, you can roll up your sleeves and figure out how to fix those systems as a team. The meeting is laid out like this:

1. **Five-Minute Opener:** First, everyone disconnects mentally from previous tasks. It's a moment to come together as a team, share professional and personal good news, and foster camaraderie.

2. **Five-Minute Scorecard Review:** Here, the team quickly reviews the metrics chosen to track progress. Are we on

track? Are we off track? It's a rapid-fire assessment to ensure everyone is aligned and aware of their goals.

3. **Five-Minute Rock Review:** This is a discussion of the individual goals that each team member has set to contribute to the office's overall objectives. Again, it's a quick check-in to see if everyone is on course or if adjustments are needed.

4. **30-minute "Meat of the Meeting:"** This is where we identify, discuss, and solve challenges. We start by identifying the systems that are broken or in need of improvement. Then, we dive deep into the discussion, prioritizing the three most critical issues to tackle using strategic problem-solving and collaboration.

As we wrap up this meeting, we take a moment to do housekeeping tasks like calendar reviews or discussing upcoming events. We also review our to-do lists. And, of course, we end on a positive note, keeping the energy upbeat and optimistic.

In addition to the IDS meeting, I recommend incorporating calibration meetings. These are smaller, more focused sessions where team members can fine-tune their skills and alignment on specific systems and procedures. Whether the back office refines tray prep for specific procedures or how to handle certain emergency situations, the front office perfects the new patient experience, or the front office discusses front office tasks, calibration meetings support ongoing learning and development in close-knit settings where the team feels supported.

Remember that meetings aren't the only component of breaking free from complacency. Your manager should be forward-thinking, practicing "servant leadership." They're the ones steering the ship in the right direction. Servant leadership involves catching your team doing things right and acknowledging their efforts. Too often, we focus on catching mistakes, but highlighting the positives is just as important. When your team feels appreciated and valued, they will likely stay engaged and motivated.

Fostering Trust and Care in a Team Environment

Several elements are involved in building a team environment that reflects trust and care among team members and extends that care to patients. These help create a cohesive atmosphere where everyone feels valued and empowered to contribute their best.

Clear Communication

At the heart of any successful team is clear and open communication. As the doctor and manager, aim to foster an environment where team members feel comfortable expressing themselves honestly. This means being able to address difficult issues head-on while always keeping the team's best interests in mind.

Shared Goals and Visions

Setting goals together as a team can be incredibly motivating and rewarding. When everyone is aligned with a common purpose, it creates a sense of unity within the practice. Each team member should understand their individual goals and how they contribute to the overarching objectives of the practice.

Team Building Activities

These activities shouldn't just be about work - they should be fun, too! Whether it's team lunches, birthday celebrations, or offsite retreats, these activities are essential for fostering camaraderie and strengthening bonds among team members.

Training and Development

Continuous investment in the development of your team is vital for maintaining a competitive edge. New employees join the team, and existing team members need opportunities to enhance their skills and knowledge. Practices demonstrate their commitment to their team's growth and success by providing training, workshops, and development opportunities.

Patient-Centered Care

Empathy, compassion, and communication are at the heart of patient-centered care. Treat patients with the respect and dignity they deserve, understand their unique needs and preferences, and provide personalized care. For example, not all moms want their children to have fluoride treatments, so meeting patients where they are is very important.

Celebrating milestones and connecting with patients fosters trust and loyalty, which is invaluable in building long-lasting relationships. For example, I once worked with a practice that would keep a daily list of patients who were getting married, retiring, just cleared from cancer, or any other notable milestones. Then, they would all sign and send a card to connect with those patients.

Simple things like this that are easily implemented can make a lasting impact.

A Culture Redefined

Let me share a story perfectly illustrating the power of investing in a team's growth and fostering a supportive, goal-oriented practice culture. It's a story of transformation, where dedication, empathy, and effective leadership turned a struggling dental office into a successful one.

A big company owner asked me to come in and see if I could apply private practice principles to his larger office. The managing doctor was not invested in the team, just in patient care. It was an issue of "herd mentality," where he was only concerned with getting these patients in and out as fast as he could. He wanted me to help improve this team and its dynamics. It was a huge mountain to climb, but they allowed me to do what needed to be done.

The journey began with a daunting task - replacing a manager whose approach had contributed to the negative office culture. Stepping into her shoes was intimidating, but I knew that change was necessary for the team to thrive. I started by talking to each team member individually, gaining insights into their perspectives and concerns. Every morning, I made it a point to personally greet every team member, setting the day's tone with positivity and recognition. Then, I organized team meetings focused on identifying and addressing the issues holding the team back. We implemented a system to measure patient satisfaction and set internal goals and metrics to improve the patient experience.

The most significant change was my leadership style. I adopted an open-door policy, inviting team members to freely share their thoughts and concerns. This newfound sense of transparency and trust encouraged team members to come forward with their ideas and suggestions. Morale improved as we made strategic changes, such as reassigning team members to roles better suited to their strengths and interests. I made a conscious effort to uplift and motivate the team, starting each meeting with activities to remind them of their value and potential.

Over time, the office culture underwent a remarkable transformation. What was once a place of discontent and frustration became a supportive environment where team members felt heard, valued, and empowered. It wasn't an overnight change, but after a year of dedicated effort, the results spoke for themselves. We saw improvements in patient satisfaction scores and productivity metrics, catapulting the office from the bottom to the top third of the group. It was a testament to the power of servant leadership, a doctor's open mind and willingness to make a change, effective communication, and genuine care for the team's well-being.

As demonstrated by the story above, it's okay if you don't have all the answers. What matters most is acknowledging a problem and taking proactive steps to address it. Don't hesitate to seek guidance and support when needed, and always prioritize your team's and patients' well-being above all else. You can shape a thriving practice culture with dedication, collaboration, and a commitment to continuous improvement.

KEY TAKEAWAYS

➲ Practice culture is the foundation of your dental office's success, influencing every patient interaction.

➲ Complacency poses a threat to positive practice culture and must be actively combated through continuous improvement efforts.

➲ Regular team meetings, such as IDS sessions, are essential for identifying and solving challenges collaboratively.

➲ Servant leadership fosters an environment where team members feel valued and motivated.

➲ Clear communication, shared goals, team-building activities, and ongoing training are vital elements for building trust and care within the team and extending it to patients.

LINDA KANE

CHAPTER THREE

THE NEW PATIENT EXPERIENCE

The new patient experience is the cornerstone of your practice's success, impacting your immediate revenue and your long-term growth potential. In this chapter, we will explore the skills and strategies needed to nurture, engage, and build rapport with new patients, ensuring they feel valued and understood from the moment they make that initial call. The new patient experience is your opportunity to showcase your practice's values and commitment to patient care. I've witnessed firsthand the transformative power of a well-executed new patient strategy. Without a steady flow of new patients, it becomes challenging for dental offices to thrive and reach their full potential.

Connecting Through the First Call

One key component of an effective new patient strategy is handling those initial phone calls. Far too often, the front desk team defaults to simply answering the caller's questions without recognizing the opportunity to engage and build rapport. Instead, I advocate for a more proactive approach that empowers the front desk team member to take control of the conversation while prioritizing the caller's needs.

When a prospective patient calls your office with questions, it's easy to fall into the trap of providing quick answers and moving on. Encourage your front desk team to acknowledge the caller's question, but then gently redirect the conversation by requesting their name and number. This allows you to maintain control of the call and lays the foundation for more personalized interaction.

Asking open-ended questions and actively listening to the caller's responses demonstrates a genuine interest in their well-being. This simple act of engagement fosters trust and sets the stage for a more meaningful patient-provider relationship.

Effective communication doesn't end with the front desk—it extends to every team member. By sharing insights and best practices across your practice, you create a unified approach to patient care that prioritizes consistency and excellence. Remember, the new patient experience is a team effort, and by working together, you can make every patient feel valued and respected.

Mastering Scheduling for New Patients

One of the most critical skills in scheduling new patients is the ability to allocate dedicated time slots specifically for them. Block scheduling offers a practical solution to this challenge by reserving

LINDA KANE

openings in the schedule for new patients in the morning and afternoon. This guarantees timely appointments for individuals seeking care, preventing them from seeking services elsewhere due to scheduling delays.

In addition to accommodating new patients, practices must prioritize flexibility for urgent cases, particularly those with severe periodontal issues or for those who are in pain. It's essential to have the flexibility to schedule these patients promptly to address their immediate needs and prevent further complications. By incorporating these urgent cases into the block scheduling system, practices can ensure that no patient is left waiting for essential care. Long wait times for new patients can harm a practice's reputation and growth. Patients unable to secure timely appointments may seek services elsewhere, leading to lost revenue and potential long-term patient relationships.

Many practices appoint a dedicated new patient coordinator to manage block scheduling. This individual is responsible for overseeing the allocation of time slots for new patients, adding blocks to the schedule for the entire year, and adjusting as needed.

The Breakfast Dilemma

When it comes to scheduling, I often draw inspiration from a familiar scenario: the chaos of a busy morning trying to get children fed and off to school. Think back to your childhood or perhaps your experience as a parent. On a hectic school morning or before heading out to church, did you or your parents offer a buffet of breakfast options, including pancakes, eggs, bacon, sausage, muffins, oatmeal, granola bars, bananas, apples, and yogurt? The answer is likely a resounding no. Instead, we offer this or that, what we have in our cupboard or fridge, what works for us!

Just as parents don't offer an endless array of breakfast options, dental practices shouldn't overwhelm patients with a multitude of scheduling choices. Instead, you should adopt the mindset of a parent, offering only what fits within your schedule and capabilities. This "mom or dad" approach means presenting patients with two choices that align with your available time slots—nothing more, nothing less.

When scheduling appointments, qualify patients and offer them options that fit their criteria. For example, if a patient indicates that Tuesday afternoons work best for them, you should focus on presenting available time slots for Tuesday afternoons. Narrow the options to fit the patient's preferences to streamline the decision-making process and avoid overwhelming them with unnecessary details. Ultimately, your goal as a dental professional is to guide patients toward appointments that match with your schedule and practice priorities.

Online Scheduling

Convenience has become an expectation in our fast-paced society. From banking to grocery shopping, most of our daily tasks can be completed with a few taps on our smartphones. Dentistry is no exception. As a dental professional, you must recognize the importance of streamlining online scheduling to meet the needs of your patients.

With dental software continually evolving, many opportunities exist to integrate online scheduling functionality into your practice. Whether through updates to their existing software or third-party solutions like Dental Intelligence, RevenueWell, Lighthouse 360, etc., practices can leverage technology to make scheduling appointments as easy as possible for patients.

Guiding Patients with Care

When triaging pain patients over the phone or online, it's crucial to approach each interaction with efficiency and empathy. As I often emphasize, every patient call begins with a question—a signal of their need for assistance and guidance. Once we've established control of the call, our priority shifts to asking the right questions to assess the severity of the patient's situation while maintaining a compassionate demeanor.

At the heart of effective triage lies empathy—the ability to connect with patients on a human level and understand their concerns. A kind, empathetic voice goes a long way in reassuring patients and easing their anxieties. Ask open-ended questions and actively listen to their responses to demonstrate your commitment to their well-being and create a supportive environment where they feel heard and understood.

Use strategic questioning to gauge the severity of their symptoms and determine the appropriate course of action. Questions like "Tell me a little bit more about that" or "Is your pain persistent?" help you gather information to make informed decisions about their care. By probing for details about their symptoms, medications, and recent accidents or trauma, you can quickly identify red flags that warrant immediate attention.

For practices offering online scheduling, it's imperative to provide clear options that align with the patient's needs and the complexity of their situation. Patients can select the most appropriate option based on their symptoms and preferences by offering predefined choices such as scheduling a cleaning and checkup or booking time with the doctor for a comprehensive or emergency exam. However, recognize the limitations of online scheduling and encourage patients with more complex needs to call and speak with a member of your team directly.

Using Teamwork to Enhance the New Patient Experience

Imagine the familiar scenario of taking your child to the doctor for an ear infection or fever. From the moment you call to make an appointment to the time you arrive at the doctor's office, you find yourself repeating your child's symptoms to multiple members of the healthcare team. While each interaction is polite and professional, it leaves you feeling, "Is this team connected? Are they really concerned about my child?"

This common experience highlights the importance of effective communication and coordination within a healthcare team. In a well-functioning dental practice, every team member—from the front desk team to the clinical assistants—actively engages in the patient's care journey. I recommend taking notes from the first patient call on a colored paper that stands out. You can take this paper to the morning huddle to share information about the patient. "Doctor, this patient goes to school with your son. You can talk about that during their first appointment." This simple strategy builds a connection with the patient from the very start.

A Tale of Two Startups

I had the privilege of assisting two startup practices, each with its unique challenges and demographics. Both practices recognized the importance of prioritizing the new patient experience from the outset. With no existing patient base to rely on, they understood that their success depended on their ability to attract and retain new patients. Guided by my new patient handling guidelines, they embraced a patient-centric approach emphasizing kindness, empathy, and thoughtfulness in every interaction.

Through daily morning huddles, the entire team had the opportunity to share insights and coordinate efforts to ensure a seamless patient experience. Additionally, both practices invested in designing front lobby waiting areas that resembled cozy living rooms—spaces where patients could feel the "Three Cs" - calm, comfortable, and in control.

Despite serving vastly different communities—one in a small town in Idaho and the other in a busy tourist destination—both practices flourished by adhering to the same principles of patient-centered care. Patients quickly recognized these practices as welcoming havens where they were treated with kindness and respect, regardless of their background or circumstances.

What made the difference? It wasn't flashy marketing campaigns or cutting-edge technology—it was the simple act of treating patients like family members or close friends. The results spoke for themselves. Both practices experienced significant growth in new patient traffic, rapidly establishing themselves as trusted pillars within their respective communities.

Guidelines for Growth

Through my years of experience and passion for excellence, I've outlined a roadmap for new dental practices aiming to grow their new patient base:

- **Community Engagement and Connection:** Get involved in your community right from the start to attract new patients naturally. Attend local events, connect with city officials, and build relationships within your community. Let people tour your facility, offer to sponsor school events, and boost your social media presence with a "like and share" campaign.

- **Patient-Centric Approach:** From the very first phone call, prioritize warmth, intention, and compassion. Make every interaction a warm welcome, leaving patients excited to meet the team and experience exceptional care. It's about making them feel like family from the moment they make their first call to you and walk in the door.

- **Empowerment through Education:** Invest in initiatives like hygienist-led school programs to promote oral health awareness. Small children have fun and learn a lot through games about brushing their teeth and good and bad foods.

- **Strategic Partnerships and Planning:** Align with trusted sources, such as Profitable PPOs, and seek expert guidance when navigating insurance contracts and reimbursement negotiations. Planning strategically and partnering wisely can optimize your financial viability while delivering quality care.

By integrating these strategies into your practice culture, you'll embark on a journey of growth, fulfillment, and endless smiles. Here's to warm welcomes, empowered patients, and stand-out practices!

KEY TAKEAWAYS

➲ Prioritize building rapport and trust with new patients from the first phone call, fostering a personalized and engaging experience.

➲ Implement block scheduling to ensure timely appointments for new patients and maintain flexibility for urgent cases.

➲ Streamline scheduling options for patients by offering limited choices that align with their preferences and practice availability.

➲ Embrace online scheduling tools to meet patient expectations for convenience and accessibility.

➲ Foster teamwork and communication within the practice to deliver seamless patient care and create lasting connections.

CHAPTER FOUR

MASTERING PRACTICE MANAGEMENT

I n the hustle and bustle of a dental office, it's easy to get caught up in a reactive mindset. However, I urge you to embrace a different perspective. Your work should not be solely determined by the circumstances of the day. Instead, strive to inject intentionality into every aspect of your practice. At the core of intentional action is implementing systems, which require constant attention and refinement to remain effective.

Enhancing Team Skills and Efficiency

Before diving into training team members, you must assess the state of your practice's systems. Look for warning signs such as low collections, unfilled chairs, decreased new patient counts, or a backlog of outstanding claims. These indicators signal areas where systems are lacking or not being correctly implemented. Once you've pinpointed the systems needing attention, it's time to go deeper. Ask yourself questions like:

- "How are we handling new patient calls?"
- "Are we capturing every caller?"
- "Is our recall program robust enough?"
- "Are patients slipping through the cracks, never to return?"
- "Are treatment plans being executed with scheduled appointments and payment arrangements in place?"
- "Is someone dedicated to managing insurance claims?"

By identifying these pain points, you can tailor your efforts to address specific areas of weakness within your office. Training should not only focus on the technical aspects of your practice's systems but also on the behaviors required to manage them. Whether it's updating third-party software or refining communication protocols, providing targeted training is essential for success, which I thoroughly enjoy doing as a consultant.

Hands-On Leadership

A great leader should be in the weeds, getting their hands dirty with the team. A true leader is present in all areas, identifying where assistance is needed and actively engaging with employees to offer support. One of the benefits of hands-on leadership is the opportunity it provides to recognize and celebrate the efforts of your team members since you will know the dedication it takes firsthand.

LINDA KANE

I had a fantastic team while managing a dental office in a previous role. Since I'm well-versed in operations but not clinically trained, I made it a point to be actively involved in day-to-day operations like assisting with room cleaning, coordinating schedules to optimize efficiency, or even making calls to pharmacies or labs. Leadership isn't confined to a specific role or skill set. When you strive to be present and willing to lend a helping hand, you can break down silos between different teams within the practice. When employees see their leader actively engaging and assisting across various tasks, it creates a sense of camaraderie and unity, leading to a more cohesive work environment.

Team Input

As a leader, I firmly believe in maintaining an open-door policy to encourage transparency and collaboration. I want to create a space where employees feel empowered to openly share their ideas and concerns. These discussions, which I call "coaching sessions," serve as a platform for generating innovative solutions and driving positive change.

Rather than focusing on complaints, I encourage my team to approach me with solutions-oriented mindsets. I welcome their input if they identify a system that needs to be fixed or could be improved. However, I ask that they come prepared with 1-3 potential solutions to discuss so that we can proactively problem-solve.

Aligning the Team

One common leadership challenge in dental practices is aligning with the doctor while managing the team effectively. Leaders must navigate situations where team members may side with either the doctor or the manager, maintaining professionalism and focusing on practice development. I often see doctors confiding too much in their dental assistants. They sit knee to knee with them all day long, and sometimes, they share too much.

To overcome these challenges, I prioritize building trust with the doctor and demonstrating my commitment to supporting the team's success as a manager. Regular goal-setting sessions and alignment meetings help ensure that the doctor and the manager are on the same page regarding practice objectives and expectations. It's a collaborative effort that requires confidence, communication, and mutual respect.

Seeking Out the Good

During my coaching sessions, I often ask, "If you stand up and point your feet to the right, which way will you go? To the left? NO… To the right! You go the way your feet are planted!" Similarly, if you look for the good, you will find it! But guess what? If you look for the bad, you will find that, too. When we actively seek out the good in our employees and their performance, we cultivate an environment that breeds positivity and enthusiasm. Whether complimenting a team member on their detailed notes or a carefully performed x-ray, they will likely produce those same results again when recognized for their efforts.

In dentistry, a common issue leads to frustration and negativity in team morale, involving tension between the front and the back of the office. For example, sometimes hygienists refuse to sanitize their instruments and pass them off to the dental assistants, who become disgruntled when they feel like the hygienists aren't pulling their weight. Sometimes, the back also blames the front office for scheduling them too tight or needing clarification about the insurance coverage of treatments like fluoride or sealants.

Even in these stressful situations, try to look for the good instead of the bad. On a day when the hygienist does clean their instruments, a dental assistant should recognize the effort and say, "Thank you! I appreciate that." It will likely happen more, or at the very least, inspire a discussion about why they don't do it more often. Reframing these situations into positive interactions can spark conversations that increase teamwork and productivity. Commit to looking for the good and celebrating the contributions of your team members every day!

Applying the Concept of Servant Leadership in Your Practice

At the heart of servant leadership is the idea of fairness and transparency. Employees should have a clear understanding of what is expected of them and the office's key performance indicators. Hearing constructive criticism should never happen in a formal review unless it just happened. Reviews should be a time to set goals and provide feedback.

I often utilize tools like the DISC Guide or the 16 Personalities Assessment to ensure that each team member is positioned for success. These tools help identify individual strengths and preferences, allowing leaders to assign roles that align with each person's unique characteristics. For example, the DISC Guide will indicate if someone is more "blue" (cautions, diplomatic, exact, indulgent, objective), "red" (direct, result-oriented, decision maker, competitive), "green" (understanding, team player, patient, stable, honest) or "yellow" (charming, enthusiastic, optimistic, convincing, inspiring).

Servant leaders prioritize the needs of their team members above their agenda. Rather than following a rigid script or checklist, they adapt their approach to meet each person's individual needs. Engage in open and honest conversations and take the time to acknowledge and celebrate each member's contributions to demonstrate your commitment to understanding and supporting your team on a personal level.

Healing a Broken Team Through Servant Leadership

Let me tell you about an incredible journey with a struggling practice. When I stepped in, the team was fractured, and there was a noticeable lack of trust in the doctor's leadership. It was a tough situation; the doctor had been through several managers before me, and the atmosphere was tense.

Instead of immediately implementing changes, I took a step back. I observed, listened, and made an effort to connect with each person individually. I asked them to fill out a questionnaire, which opened up many doors for honest conversations. They had every reason to be skeptical of another new manager, so building trust was my top priority.

Once I understood the office dynamics well, I sat down with the doctor to discuss what I had found. I didn't divulge any private details but outlined the general issues I had observed. To my surprise, he was receptive and willing to make changes despite his doubts about our chances of success. Together, we made a plan. We identified areas for improvement and outlined actionable steps to get there. It was a collaborative effort; having the doctor on board was crucial to our success.

One of the first things I did was to make strategic adjustments to the team's roles and responsibilities. I moved a dental assistant to the front desk who had back problems and struggled to work chairside. I also moved the sterilization assistant to training as the doctor's new dental assistant. She was so excited for the opportunity. We implemented the New Patient Experience, which I handled. I had the new helper at the front take over the Recare Program, and the seasoned assistant helped me work on the unscheduled treatment when she had extra time. I did all the financial consults, training the team as I went. We worked together, and everyone soon learned they could trust me. We hired another front office person who took over some of the projects I did so that I could work more with treatment. And while all of these changes were being implemented, we had fun! Every Monday, I brought donuts or baked something - they loved it! The doctor started feeling the change, and he was so grateful.

Through it all, I embraced the principles of servant leadership. For me, leadership is not about being in charge but serving others and helping them succeed. By investing in my team and creating a positive work environment, we were able to turn things around and make the office a place where they truly wanted to be.

I encourage all dental practice managers to remember the power of servant leadership. Strive to lead with empathy, humility, and a genuine desire to serve others. You work for your team - not the other way around! Together, you can elevate practice excellence and achieve remarkable results.

KEY TAKEAWAYS

⮞ Implement systems in your dental practice to maintain focus and control, ensuring consistent operations and patient care.

⮞ Hands-on leadership involves leaders actively engaging with the team, building unity, and creating a positive work environment.

⮞ Encourage a solutions-based approach with an open-door policy, fostering innovation through collaboration and feedback.

⮞ Achieve team alignment by maintaining open communication with doctors and setting shared goals.

⮞ Practice servant leadership by prioritizing fairness and transparency and supporting the team with empathy and humility.

LINDA KANE

PART TWO

ATTRACTING AND KEEPING YOUR PATIENT BASE

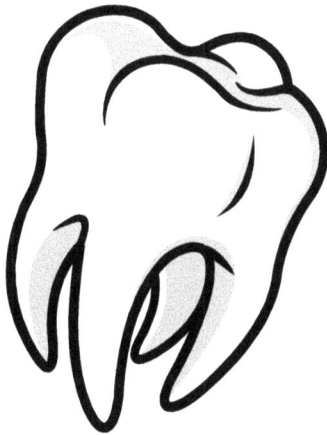

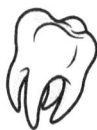

CHAPTER FIVE

YOUR IDEAL PATIENTS

When running a dental practice, a consistent flow of new patients is crucial, but retaining them is the real key to success. You might have experienced empty chairs despite having many new patients initially. Many dental professionals ask, "Why didn't 'so and so' schedule back?" This chapter focuses on creating a culture and implementing strategies that ensure people return to your office time and time again.

To understand why patients return—or don't—you must evaluate the entire patient experience, from the first phone call to the final checkout. These details shape a patient's overall experience and ultimately determine whether they will return.

Touchpoints for a Great Patient Experience

- **Appointment Scheduling:** Was the process easy? Did the front desk team communicate effectively and confirm the appointment promptly?
- **Timeliness:** Was the patient taken to the chair on time, or did they have to wait?
- **Clinical Engagement:** Did the clinical team engage with the patient? Did they seem interested in their concerns and explain procedures in a way the patient could understand?
- **Doctor Interaction:** Did the doctor or hygienist show empathy and take time to answer questions? Did they avoid "dump truck" dentistry, where too much information is given at once?
- **Checkout Process:** Was the checkout process smooth? Was the insurance estimate ready, and did the team explain it well?
- **Overall Impression:** Did the patient leave with a feeling of satisfaction, thinking, "I didn't expect that level of care?"

Team Calibration

Your team should always be on the same page to maintain a high level of patient satisfaction. I suggest monthly team calibrations, where you conduct a walkthrough of the practice as if you were a patient. Look at everything from the patient's perspective. Are the floors clean? Are there cobwebs in the corners? Is the front desk cluttered? Does the overall environment feel welcoming?

During these calibrations, break down tasks into manageable parts. Have team members role-play as patients to identify areas for improvement. This exercise helps everyone to understand the importance of creating a positive patient experience and know what it takes to achieve it.

Every patient should have a reason to come back, whether for their next cleaning, a filling, or a follow-up on a procedure. Your team should focus on scheduling the next appointment while the patient is still in the office. Don't chase them later—get them on the calendar before they leave. This proactive approach creates a steady flow of returning patients. By implementing these strategies and maintaining a patient-centric culture, you'll find that patient retention and your practice's overall success will improve.

The Morning Huddle

In a startup practice, the dependency on new patients is high, and teamwork makes them stay. We had a small team in my last office, but we were a force to be reckoned with. Our morning huddles were lively and engaging, focusing on our goals and finding opportunities to serve our patients better. We relied heavily on new patients, so we would discuss who was coming in every morning, their needs, and how we could make them feel welcome.

During these huddles, we discussed our individual and team goals. The morning huddle is truly an "opportunity finder!" The hygienist focused on offering sealants and fluoride, while the assistant promoted whitening services. The team focused on family members of patients coming in that day and whether they were due for cleanings or treatment. We discussed how we performed the day before and what we could improve. The morning huddle sets the tone for the day, allowing everyone to align their goals and discuss what needs to be achieved.

Teaching Patients About Mutual Respect and Treatment Expectations

Educating patients about the importance of their treatment and why it's necessary plays a considerable role in whether or not you will see them again. This requires effective communication and mutual respect between the dental team and the patients. I firmly believe in the 95/5 principle: 95% of the effort should go into explaining why treatment is important and only 5% into closing the deal, arranging payment, and booking the appointment. This focus on patient education helps create a sense of trust and understanding, leading to better patient compliance.

To make treatment recommendations resonate with people, frame the conversation in terms they can relate to. I often use analogies to drive the point home. For example, you wouldn't try convincing someone in Mexico to put snow tires on their vehicle. Similarly, you wouldn't try to sell a vacuum cleaner to someone with a dirt floor. If a patient doesn't see the need for treatment, they're unlikely to follow through with it.

When patients come in for an appointment, they may have preconceived notions about dentistry or not fully understand the risks of avoiding treatment. It's up to the dental team to explain why a procedure is important, what could happen if they don't proceed, and the potential outcomes. If the patient doesn't understand or feel the treatment is necessary, they will no-show their appointment or decline the procedure altogether.

To prevent this, spend time educating the patient. Explain in simple terms why a specific treatment is crucial and how it impacts their oral health. Discuss the risks of ignoring the issue and the benefits of taking action. When the patient starts to use their own words to express understanding, like saying, "Yeah, I get it," or "That makes sense," you know they've bought into the treatment plan. If they seem hesitant or unsure, step back and reframe the conversation. Sometimes, it's better not to push for an appointment if the patient isn't ready. A forced appointment might lead to a no-show, which benefits no one.

Slowing Down to Listen and Explain

In dentistry, it's easy to get caught up in the routine of day-to-day operations. But to truly connect with people, you must slow down and listen. This applies to both doctors and front-office staff. To create a positive patient experience, give patients the illusion that you have all the time in the world for them.

When you see doctors leaning back in their chairs, crossing their legs, and relaxing while talking to patients, you know they're doing it right. It's about giving the impression that you have time to listen and engage, even if there's a hygienist in the hallway flagging you for another exam. Instead of rushing through explanations, take the time to discuss what needs to be done and ask if the patient has any questions. It creates a sense of calm and shows that you're genuinely interested in their concerns.

I've often found that patients come to the front desk with questions about their procedures. This can happen for two reasons: either they were too scared or embarrassed to ask the doctor or the doctor didn't spend enough time explaining the treatment using the 95/5 principle. As a front-office team member, you need to be prepared to answer these questions, but it's also a sign that the initial consultation may need improvement.

Using Empathetic Verbiage

Words matter, especially when communicating with dental patients. Verbiage plays a huge role in explaining treatment plans and associated costs. Your language can build trust or create confusion, so I recommend breaking down the treatment plan into simple, understandable terms.

Here's an example of how I do it:

- Start with the Fees: I explain, "This column shows our office fee. This one, we know for sure." This establishes a clear baseline for what the office charges.
- Explain the Insurance Estimate: Next, I move to the insurance estimate, saying, "This column is what we estimate your insurance might cover. This is based on the information we've received from your insurance company." The use of words like "estimate," "might," and "believe" indicates that this is not a solid number and could change.
- Identify the Patient's Out-of-Pocket Cost: Finally, I explain the difference between the office fee and the estimated insurance coverage, stating, "This is the math problem—the difference between our fee and what we believe your insurance might cover." You set realistic expectations when you acknowledge this uncertainty.

After explaining the costs, I use a phrase that has proven successful in engaging patients: "So this would be your out-of-pocket estimate for this treatment. How would you like to take care of this today?" At this point, I give a friendly smile and make eye contact without saying anything else. This silence allows the patient to start problem-solving on their own, often leading them to consider their payment options.

Many dental practices have software that allows you to print treatment plans with financial options. Predetermine these options and point out the different choices available when discussing costs. This additional flexibility can help people feel more at ease about their financial obligations.

Feedback for Continuous Improvement

Gathering feedback from patients is a valuable tool in identifying areas for improvement and implementing changes that enhance patient experiences. In my experience, sending out surveys is a great way to collect this information. However, be selective about who you send these surveys to. You don't want to send them exclusively to the angriest patients but rather to a diverse group that can provide constructive feedback. Once you've collected feedback, bring it back to the team for discussion. I recommend integrating the feedback into your Identify, Discuss, and Solve (IDS) sessions. This process allows you to improve your practice, enhancing patient satisfaction continuously.

Managing No-Shows and Late Cancellations

One of a dental practice's biggest headaches is dealing with no-shows and late cancellations. This problem affects every doctor, so here are some strategies that can help address this issue.

- **Importance of Patient Buy-In:** First, let's go back to the 95/5 principle. Patients who don't understand or value the treatment are less likely to attend their appointments. This lack of buy-in is a significant cause of no-shows. To mitigate this, ensure that you spend adequate time educating patients about why their treatment is important.

- **Appointment Cards with Clear Expectations:** Another protocol to help manage no-shows and cancellations is stating appointment card expectations clearly. A simple phrase like, "This time is specially reserved for you. Kindly provide 48 hours' notice if you're unable to keep the appointment" can set the tone. But it's not enough to print it on the card; you need to emphasize it verbally when giving it to the patient. Highlight the words and gently remind them that a 48-hour notice is required if they need to cancel. This approach helps patients understand that their time is valuable, and so is yours.

- **Automated Appointment Reminders:** Most dental practices use third-party software to send text reminders at intervals, like a month before the appointment, two weeks before, and the day before. These automated texts are convenient for patients, allowing them to confirm their appointments easily. If they confirm, the reminders stop, but if they don't, your team should follow up with a phone call to keep the appointment on their radar.

- **Handling Day-of Cancellations:** Now, let's talk about what to do when a patient calls to cancel on the day of their appointment. This is where you need to get your "mom voice" ready. If you've given them all the reminders and they still try to cancel at the last minute, it's time to express concern in a firm but caring way. When a patient calls to cancel, respond with, "Oh, I'm so sorry. Are you sure there's no way to make it? We really want to see you. If you cancel now, the next available appointment might take a while. Is there really no way to make it work?" This approach puts the ball back in their court, and they often reconsider. If you say, "Okay, thanks for letting us know. Do you want to reschedule?" without emphasizing the inconvenience, they'll think it's okay to do it again.

Managing no-shows and late cancellations requires patient education, clear communication, and a touch of firmness when needed. The goal is to establish a culture where patients understand the value of their appointments and the impact their cancellation has on the practice.

Patient Engagement

A positive patient experience goes beyond just clinical treatment; it's about creating a welcoming environment where people feel at ease. In our practice, we had a unique way of connecting with patients. We had pictures of our dogs on the wall with their nameplates, and when we gave new patients a tour of the office, they'd always chuckle at the sight. This little touch warmed the atmosphere and made people feel at home.

When patients left, we wanted them to have a smile on their faces, so we always made sure they felt appreciated and valued. During their visit, we would discuss family, pets, or hobbies, creating a personal connection. By having an effective morning huddle and focusing on teamwork, we became a well-oiled machine, providing excellent care while keeping things fun and engaging. Ultimately, the key to a successful dental practice is creating an environment where both the team and the patients enjoy coming in. If it's not fun, it's not worth it.

Loyalty Programs

You need to tread carefully when it comes to reward systems or loyalty programs in dental practices. If you're under contract with a patient's insurance, rewarding them for visiting your office or referring others could breach your contract, leading to legal troubles. Many doctors might not know this, but it's a risk you don't want to take.

However, there are ways to create loyalty programs that are both effective and compliant with the rules. These are generally designed for patients who don't have dental insurance, allowing them to build their own in-house plan that offers a variety of benefits. You can call it a "VIP Program," "Patient Loyalty Program," or "Patient Savings Plan."

If you're considering a loyalty program, one common approach is to create a plan that allows people without dental insurance to pay an annual fee. In return, they receive free cleanings, X-rays, exams, and a discount on additional treatments—typically around 15%.

Consider offering different tiers for your program. For instance, if you have periodontal patients who require more frequent cleanings, you can create a plan that accommodates their needs. This could include four cleanings a year, X-rays, exams, and a discount on other treatments. Offering a plan with multiple tiers allows you to cater to different patient needs while maintaining compliance with insurance regulations.

Another way to build a loyalty program is to implement a subscription-based model. In this approach, patients pay a monthly fee—say, $35—and in return, they get access to a reduced fee schedule for various treatments. This subscription fee can add up over time, allowing patients to "bank" their payments to cover future treatments at a discounted rate. This subscription model is flexible and cost-effective for people to manage dental care without traditional insurance, which can be especially appealing during economic uncertainty when people are looking for affordable healthcare options.

Before implementing any loyalty program, consult with legal counsel or a compliance expert to ensure you're on the right track. It's also a good idea to communicate clearly with your staff about the specifics of your program so they understand who is eligible and what benefits are included. As you think about implementing a loyalty program, remember the importance of compliance and patient education. Balancing these elements creates a program that supports your patients' needs while ensuring your practice stays within the boundaries of insurance contracts and regulations.

Community Engagement

Even a small practice can make a big impact in its community by getting involved with local schools. You have a unique opportunity to educate young children about oral health in a fun and memorable way. In my last practice, we reached out to preschools and elementary schools, offering to teach kids about dental hygiene. It's a great way to make an impression on the children and their parents.

We created a simple but engaging lesson plan. We made a large board shaped like a tooth and laminated pictures of various foods. The kids loved it because they got to decide if the foods were "good" or "bad" for their teeth. Apples, bananas, and other fruits received thumbs up, while candy and raisins received thumbs down.

These sessions are a win-win: educate children about oral health, and your practice gains visibility. At the end of each session, we handed out goodie bags containing small toothbrushes and those little pink tablets to chew on that show where plaque builds up on your teeth. We also included information about our practice. Engaging with schools doesn't require a lot of effort or resources. You don't need a complicated setup; call the local schools and ask if they'd like a visit from a dentist or hygienist to talk about dental hygiene. Most schools welcome these educational sessions, often seeking guest speakers to engage with the children. We found that showing up in our scrubs with a bag of goodies was enough to make an impact. The kids loved it, and the teachers appreciated the break in their routine. Plus, parents usually take notice when kids bring home something from school. This simple strategy can go a long way in building your practice's reputation within the community.

In addition to engaging with schools, get involved in the broader community. Joining the local Chamber of Commerce is a great start, as it connects you with other businesses and provides opportunities to participate in community events. In my practice, we were always involved in community-sponsored events, whether a Christmas parade or a local festival.

Being active in the community helps you stand out from other practices. There were six other dentists in our town, but none of them participated in these events. We made it a point to be present, and it paid off. Although it requires a small investment, the return on community involvement is significant.

A Patient-Centric Culture

As you explore different ways to engage and retain patients, remember that when treated with love, compassion, empathy, and respect, they feel the culture you've created and want to be a part of it. This simple concept has a ripple effect that can transform a dental practice. Each interaction with a patient is an opportunity to create a positive experience that encourages loyalty and trust. You build a foundation for a thriving, patient-centric culture by teaching patients how to treat you through your actions and words.

A patient-centric culture doesn't happen by accident—it requires intention, effort, and a genuine commitment to caring for the people you serve. Embrace these strategies to create a space where patients feel valued, respected, and eager to return. This leads to improved patient retention, better treatment plan compliance, and a more successful dental practice.

KEY TAKEAWAYS

➲ Patient retention is as crucial as attracting new patients. A great patient experience, from the initial phone call to the final checkout, creates a culture where people want to return.

➲ Team calibration and effective morning huddles ensure consistent, patient-focused service. These practices keep everyone on the same page and help identify areas for improvement by seeing things from the patient's perspective.

➲ Educating patients about their treatment is key to retention. The 95/5 principle emphasizes patient education to build trust, leading to better compliance and fewer no-shows.

➲ Clear communication and empathetic verbiage improve the patient experience. Simplifying treatment plans, providing clear cost estimates, and giving patients time to process payment options contribute to a positive environment.

➲ Community engagement and compliant loyalty programs help boost visibility and attract patients. Activities like school visits and Chamber of Commerce events create a welcoming environment, encouraging people to return.

LINDA KANE

CHAPTER SIX

CASE ACCEPTANCE

C ase acceptance is one of the top five systems in the front office and is a huge contributor to a dental practice's revenue cycle. When doctors meet with patients, they prioritize showing compassion and explaining the necessary treatments. They diagnose the treatment and rely on the front office team to "have their back" by ensuring the plan is scheduled and implemented. This chapter will cover the techniques that can lead to successful case presentations and case acceptance, as well as the factors contributing to lost cases.

To present treatment plans effectively, let's start with the fundamental concept I explained in Chapter Five, the 95/5 principle. If the clinical team has prepared the patient well, educated them about their treatment needs, and reached their agreement, then 95% of the work is done. The final 5% is where the case presentation and acceptance process comes into play.

Consider the analogy of purchasing a car. When you buy a car, you take it for a test drive, discuss it with your companion, and agree to make the purchase. The salesperson takes you to a little room, reviews the numbers, getting you the best detail they can! Eventually they hand you the keys and that envelope with the rolled up papers! Then you are on your way! It's an exciting experience that culminates with you driving off in your new car.

That's precisely how case presentations should work in a dental practice. The patient should leave with a signed treatment plan, financial plan, and an appointment in the books. One of the biggest mistakes you can make is handing a patient a pamphlet and saying, "Let me know if this works for you." A successful case presentation guides the patient through the process with empathy and compassion, addressing any concerns and making sure they feel confident moving forward with the treatment. This way, you've achieved case acceptance, and they leave the office excited about their next appointment, not confused or doubtful.

The Role of Patient Education in Case Acceptance

Patient education is critical in the treatment planning and consultation process and aligns with our 95/5 principle. Doctors must create an environment where patients feel like they have time to discuss their concerns.

It's also important to anticipate questions that patients may not even know they have. Addressing these questions can guide them toward understanding their treatment needs. Show them physically—point out the areas of concern on their X-rays or intraoral photos. Display the big dark spots, explain their meaning, and why they could be problematic. Use printed images and circle the concerning areas to make the explanation interactive.

Visual aids are powerful in patient education. Showing a patient where the decay is and how a problem spot could lead to significant issues creates a sense of urgency. You can even use analogies to make the concepts relatable. For example, comparing a dental issue to a noise in a car—if you catch it early, it's a cheap fix, but if you let it go, it becomes much more expensive. This comparison resonates with people and helps them understand the importance of timely treatment.

Strategies for Addressing Patient Objections

Often, objections arise because the initial consult didn't cover enough ground, leading to what I referred to in Chapter Five as "dump truck dentistry." This occurs when a doctor unloads an extensive treatment plan on the patient and sends them to the front desk to finalize the details. Selling the plan is much more challenging when the patient is overwhelmed and confused. If an office has someone conducting the financial consult with clinical experience or someone who's been around the block a few times, they might be able to save the situation by showing empathy and concern, showing areas on the X-rays, and explaining the areas of concern that the doctor mentioned.

However, if there's real pushback, it's better to refrain from proceeding with the financial consultation. Instead, consider scheduling the patient to return for a more detailed discussion with the doctor. This allows them to ask more questions and for the doctor to explain the treatment plan more thoroughly. This is especially important when presenting large cases that require much more commitment from the patient.

Addressing objections requires clear communication and a unified approach from the dental team. It's important to show compassion and empathy when addressing these objections. Recognize the signs of "dump truck dentistry" and know when to reestablish the consultation to guide patients toward understanding and ultimately increase case acceptance.

Leveraging Financing Options for Increased Case Acceptance

Financing plays a significant role in case acceptance, especially when 68% of Americans live paycheck to paycheck. Despite this, many dental practices tend to offer in-house payment plans or traditional credit options or place themselves in the position of a bank. This can be a dangerous game. When practices loan money to patients over long periods, expecting small monthly payments of $50 or $100, it can become a debilitating financial burden. Similarly, while services like CareCredit are widely accepted across various industries, including veterinary, optometry, and general medicine, they can be among the most expensive options for dentists. So, to avoid these pitfalls, think of financial arrangements as a tool belt—a set of versatile options that can adapt to each patient's unique needs:

- **Math and Insurance:** Begin by breaking down the costs. Explain the total treatment cost, the estimated insurance contribution, and the estimated out-of-pocket portion. This approach helps patients understand the financial scope and plan accordingly.

- **Down Payments and Flexible Options:** Recognize that most people dislike down payments. Flexible financing options allow patients to choose what works best for their budget. Establishing a clear financial policy beforehand ensures smooth discussions with patients about their options. Among the choices available are Alphaeon, SunBit, Cherry, United Credit, Momnt, or Proceed, which are tailored to meet individual financial preferences.

Remember that verbiage makes all the difference. After explaining the cost breakdown, ask patients how they would like to take care of this today? This question encourages them to start problem-solving and considering their financial choices. Show them the treatment plan with the available financing options, and let them choose the one that best suits their needs.

The Black Plastic Bag

One key lesson I've learned in my career is that you should never make assumptions about patients, especially regarding their financial situations. In one of my first practices, we had a patient who came in every year for his cleaning. He objected to coming every six months, so he settled for an annual visit. He didn't see the need to act despite repeated warnings about the treatment he needed. He was a hardworking cowboy, always covered in dirt from his farm work.

One day, he came in for his appointment with a toothache. The doctor diagnosed that the tooth was too far gone, confirming our earlier warnings. Now, he had two options: either do a bridge to replace the missing tooth or get an implant. Both are expensive, but the implant takes longer and costs more, while the bridge affects the teeth on either side. It's a significant decision to make.

When he came to my desk for a financial consultation, with his muck boots leaving a mud trail through the office, I reviewed the treatment plan with him, discussing the costs and options and expecting him to choose the cheaper bridge option. But what happened next surprised me. He pulled out the corner of a black plastic bag and took out $10,000 in $100 bills. He was ready to pay for the implant in cash.

I had the best time that day, scheduling his treatment and getting him sorted out. He knew he had waited too long, letting the problem escalate to the point where it required an extraction and a complex implant procedure. Despite this, he accepted responsibility and was ready to move forward. It was a great moment, not just because he paid in full but because he was taking ownership of his oral health and doing what he needed to do.

This story reminds us never to judge a book by its cover. Just because someone looks a certain way or has a particular lifestyle doesn't mean they can't afford the treatment. Always approach patients with an open mind and never make assumptions regarding their financial situation. You never know who might surprise you with a black plastic bag full of cash, ready to invest in their dental health.

Meeting Patients Where They Are

Another unique experience that taught me the importance of meeting patients where they are, without judgment or preconceptions, happened in one of my last offices. A prisoner who was nearing the end of his sentence came in. He arrived in street clothes but with a guard by his side. The sight of him intimidated my team—they stayed in the back, hesitant to come forward—but I was alone at the front desk, and he was 30 minutes early for his appointment.

I decided to talk to him, so I started a conversation, and we ended up having one of the best chats I've ever had. I even asked him about his tattoos, which can be a sensitive topic, but he was more than happy to share. He approached the desk and showed me his tattoos, explaining how some were difficult to get, and others had significant meaning to him. It was a fascinating conversation, and I strongly connected with him.

I knew he was probably nervous about how he would be received in a dental office, so I took the time to make him feel comfortable. As we talked, I learned he had saved money while in prison because he knew he had a lot of dental treatment to get done. He'd been in fights, had some broken teeth, and needed serious dental work. I realized that taking the time to talk to him helped him feel at ease and built trust.

During our conversation, he mentioned that he loved to bake. This struck me because I had recently entered a contest to bake cookies for a local shop. I started my Zeroed-In Dental Solutions business by baking cookies and delivering flyers to dental offices. When I mentioned this to him, he offered to come over and make the dough for me once he got out of prison because he knew I was busy. I was touched by his offer.

Many would have judged this patient for his past, but he became a lifelong friend. He changed his life around, and I'm glad I treated him with compassion instead of assumptions. It was a reminder that our role in dentistry is not just to fix teeth; it's also about building relationships and understanding the people behind the smiles.

When it comes to case acceptance, the key is to meet people where they are and be prepared for their unique situations. Patients are not a one-size-fits-all group; everyone has a different story. Being flexible and adaptable is crucial, but you must approach every patient empathetically. Dental treatment can be a daunting experience for many people, and it's our job to make it as comfortable as possible.

Never let the patient leave without addressing their needs to prevent further discomfort, pain, or more severe issues. Take care of the patient while they're in the office to show that you genuinely care about their well-being. Don't just focus on getting them in and out without a plan. This approach builds trust and increases the likelihood of case acceptance.

Whether dealing with a prisoner about to re-enter society or a hardworking farmer with a black plastic bag full of cash, the approach remains the same: be empathetic and adaptable and ensure they leave with a sense of resolution. By following these principles, your dental practice becomes a place where patients feel valued, respected, and, most importantly, cared for.

KEY TAKEAWAYS

➲ Successful case acceptance relies on effective case presentations, where patients feel confident about their treatment plan and leave the office with a clear understanding of the next steps.

➲ Patient education is a crucial aspect of the treatment planning process, requiring doctors to create an environment where patients feel comfortable asking questions and discussing concerns.

➲ Addressing objections involves clear communication and avoiding "dump truck dentistry," where patients are overwhelmed with information. When objections arise, it's better to reestablish the consultation process.

➲ A solid tool belt for financial consultations includes financing options to meet patient needs and avoiding in-house payment plans that could burden the practice financially.

➲ Never judge patients based on appearances or assumptions about their financial situation. Always approach them with empathy and compassion, ensuring they leave with a sense of resolution and a plan in place.

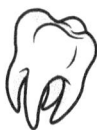

CHAPTER SEVEN

FOLLOW UP AND CONTINUOUS CARE

F ollowing up on patient care is a courtesy and a necessity for sustaining and growing a dental practice. I once heard, "Numbers that aren't tracked don't happen." Without follow-ups on continued hygiene appointments or specific treatments, you miss opportunities to keep your practice thriving. Remember, you need butts in the chairs to make the money that keeps your ship afloat.

One thing that keeps patients coming back is reliable systems and the people who implement them. Consider the example of a Starbucks cup, which features six boxes on the side for decaf, shots, syrup, milk, custom, and drink. This setup allows for countless drink combinations, representing a system that facilitates efficiency and customization. However, the system itself doesn't operate independently; it requires a person to check the right boxes and know the recipes that can be created from those options.

In dentistry, the scenario is quite similar. We have systems for virtually every aspect of practice management—from team meetings and employee reviews to supply ordering, case acceptance, hygiene retention, marketing, sterilization, leadership, OSHA safety, the new patient experience, collections, insurance, and teamwork. These systems are designed to streamline operations and enhance efficiency but do not operate in a vacuum. They need dedicated people responsible for their implementation and maintenance, ensuring each system is well-oiled and functioning correctly. Systems run the practice, but people run the systems. When a system is underperforming, the response should never be to attack the person; instead, focus on improving the system to create better outcomes.

The Cost of Missed Opportunities

In dental practices, the absence of systems can lead to significant financial losses, essentially turning operations into a money pit. This often stems from missed treatment and hygiene scheduling opportunities. It's usually too easy for practices to become complacent, focusing only on the day's immediate tasks and neglecting the bigger picture.

A common question among dentists revolves around generating additional income beyond typical procedures like crowns and implants. The answer often lies not in expanding services but in optimizing existing systems within the practice. Effective systems help prevent the usual reactive mode of operation, such as gathering insurance information post-treatment or dealing with claim rejections due to incomplete data or inadequate diagnostic images.

With the correct systems in place, you can ensure that all necessary information and documentation are collected upfront, significantly reducing the frequency of claim rejections and accelerating the payment process.

Practices should adopt a proactive rather than reactive approach, which includes:

1. Collecting insurance details correctly before providing services.
2. Ensuring that all diagnostic requirements like X-rays and intraoral camera photos are taken before submitting claims.
3. Keeping thorough and accurate treatment notes to avoid the need for amendments, which can appear suspicious and risk claim denials.

Many dental practices overlook the resources already at their disposal that can be optimized for better financial outcomes. Ask yourself these questions:

- Are fee schedules with insurance providers up-to-date and reflective of the most beneficial terms?
- Are claims being submitted correctly the first time to avoid backlogs and unnecessary write-offs?
- Is the new patient experience managed well to ensure a steady influx of new clients?
- Is there a robust recall program in place to keep patients returning regularly?
- How effective is the case acceptance rate, and are treatments scheduled and paid for promptly?
- Is the front office efficiently collecting payments at the time of service?

By shifting focus from merely handling daily tasks to optimizing and leveraging existing systems, practices can uncover significant hidden revenue opportunities within their current operations.

Persistence Pays Off

When a patient does not immediately schedule a treatment, it might be due to a lack of understanding or immediate buy-in. Therefore, it is essential to continually remind them of the treatment they need. This persistent follow-up serves two purposes: it is an act of caring that can prevent further discomfort for the patient, and it also helps in optimizing the practice's operations by filling schedule gaps and ensuring treatments are not indefinitely postponed.

Every dentist's primary goal is to prevent pain and improve the quality of life for their patients. This is why dentists often put a "watch" on a tooth, indicating a concern but opting to monitor the situation. However, once a treatment is deemed necessary, prompt action becomes critical. Just as we would address a car's unusual noise before it turns into a costly repair, addressing dental issues early can prevent more severe and expensive treatments down the line. A simple cavity left unattended can eventually require a root canal or a crown or even lead to an extraction and implant.

Personal Touch in Patient Follow-Ups

The best follow-up strategies start with personal engagement, especially with regular appointments like hygiene visits. When hygienists meet patients, I advise writing down personal details about their lives during their visit. This information is referenced in future

LINDA KANE

appointments, enhancing personal connection and making people feel valued and remembered.

Due to their frequent interactions with patients, hygienists play a large role in managing recall appointments. They often have a better rapport with patients than dentists, usually seen only for more urgent needs. It is more natural for hygienists to handle the scheduling of recall appointments. It feels personal to the patient and leverages the trust and relationship built by the hygienist. If a hygienist is running late, they can coordinate with the front office to get the patient's next appointment scheduled, maintaining continuity of care.

This personal approach also requires a structured recall program to be truly effective. It ensures that patients do not fall through the cracks and helps the practice maintain a steady flow of appointments. A recall program employing various communication methods can significantly enhance re-engagement rates. I don't recommend relying solely on traditional methods like postcards since many people don't even open their mail. A rotational communication strategy that includes texts, calls, emails, and physical mail can cater to different patient preferences and increase the effectiveness of the recall efforts.

Software Solutions

We live in a world of automation. Back in the day, we didn't even have cell phones, but now everything is available at our fingertips, so take advantage of it! I've encountered practices clinging to older systems with manual, labor-intensive processes for managing patient follow-ups. The teams had to physically print lists of patients due for recall, handwrite messages, make individual calls, and then manually enter notes back into the system—often forgetting to do so. This method was not only time-consuming but also full of inefficiencies and errors. These practices struggled with follow-up delays, missed opportunities for re-engagement, and a noticeable impact on operational productivity.

Another practice where I consulted had embraced modern dental software—Open Dental—paired with a third-party engagement and communication system. Those would be software options like iCore Connect, Dental Intelligence, Revenue Well, etc. This setup transformed their follow-up process dramatically. The software allowed the team to effortlessly pull up lists of patients based on specific criteria, such as those with remaining insurance benefits or those needing particular treatments. With a few clicks, the system enabled the team to send mass texts for appointment reminders, billing, or special calls to action, like filling in last-minute openings in the dentist's schedule.

For example, if a sudden slot was available on a Tuesday and the system identified patients who preferred appointments on that day and had pending treatments, it could automatically send targeted messages to them. This approach saved precious time and significantly enhanced patient response rates. Payments were made easier as people could settle their bills directly through a link sent via text, allowing them to pay via methods they use every day! This leads to quicker revenue collection. As I often say, "Boom diggity, money in the bank."

A well-chosen system allows practices to act on data effectively, streamline operations, and enhance patient communications. The key is not just to collect data but to dynamically use it to make informed decisions and take action.

Analyzing Data

While each dental software might offer different reports, the underlying data and what it represents remain consistent across platforms. I recommend tracking these key performance indicators:

- **Production and Adjusted Production**
  Adjusted production takes into account insurance company write-offs, providing a clearer picture of what the practice actually earns. This metric helps practices gauge whether they meet daily production goals and manage insurance write-offs properly.

- **Collection Rates**
  One of the most telling indicators of a practice's financial health is its collection rate compared to adjusted production. I remember when a doctor knelt beside my chair and discussed categorizing collection rates into grades. He said, "Linda, if your collections are 98 to 100% of my adjusted production, you will get an A. If they are 97% of my adjusted production, you will get a B," and so forth. I learned that the standard for a financially healthy office was collecting 96 to 100% of the doctor's adjusted production.

- **Management of Outstanding Claims**
  Keeping track of outstanding claims, especially those over 90 days, is necessary for maintaining cash flow and operational efficiency. Long-term outstanding claims should be kept to a minimum, dominated by secondary insurance or orthodontic claims. Recent challenges, such as cybersecurity breaches affecting healthcare, may cause fluctuations. Still,

the goal should typically be to maintain specific percentages across various time frames, ensuring that most claims are cleared within 30 days.

- **Recall Efficiency**
  Another area to monitor is the recall system—specifically, how many patients scheduled for recall are actually booking follow-up appointments. This metric reflects how well the practice manages patient re-engagement and the performance of the hygiene team in encouraging patients to return.

- **Case Acceptance Rates**
  Tracking case acceptance rates gives insight into how many proposed treatments are converted into scheduled appointments. This is a direct indicator of patient trust and the effectiveness of the practice's communication regarding the value and necessity of treatments.

Managing a dental practice's follow-up and continuous care revolves around the people who bring your systems to life. Your practice can operate seamlessly when people understand their roles and are supported and valued. It requires a blend of sophisticated systems, detailed performance tracking, and an empowered and knowledgeable team. Focusing on these areas helps practices meet and exceed operational and patient care goals.

LINDA KANE

KEY TAKEAWAYS

⮥ Implementing systems in dental practices streamlines operations and enhances efficiency, but these systems require dedicated team members to function effectively and avoid becoming financial drains due to missed opportunities.

⮥ Proactive management strategies, including proper insurance and diagnostic preparations, can optimize existing resources and systems within the practice to reduce claim rejections and improve financial outcomes.

⮥ Persistent follow-up with patients demonstrates care and concern, preventing further discomfort, but it also fills scheduling gaps and ensures that treatments do not get indefinitely postponed.

⮥ Leveraging software solutions and automation, such as Open Dental paired with CRM systems, transforms patient follow-up processes, increases engagement, and ensures timely collections.

⮥ Regular performance tracking through key indicators like collections efficiency and case acceptance rates empowers practices to gauge effectiveness, adjust strategies, and achieve optimal operational and patient care goals.

PART THREE

BOOM DIGGITY, MONEY IN THE BANK

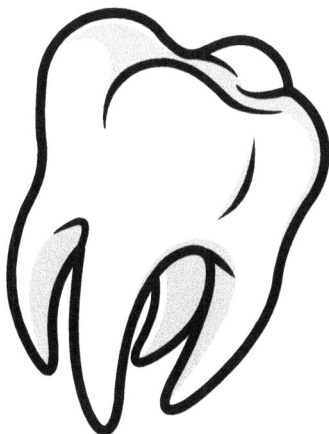

CHAPTER EIGHT

SIMPLIFYING THE ACCOUNTS RECEIVABLE PROCESS

Without an accounts receivable system, things can quickly go awry, jeopardizing your practice's financial health. Many dental office teams think sending statements is sufficient, but systems and processes are requirements for robust revenue optimization. It's foundational—something you can't afford to overlook.

Before we get into the ins and outs of a patient billing system, it's vital to grasp one essential component: collecting at the time of service. Remember our discussions on case presentations? The financial agreements made there should be non-negotiable. For instance, if a patient agrees to make payments, those should be automatically charged to their card on the pre-agreed dates. This method prevents the all-too-common scenario of chasing down payments after the fact. It's much simpler to collect from a patient while they're still in your office than to try to secure payment after they've left. That's why I always recommend reviewing tomorrow's schedule today. Check if anyone has a past-due balance and address it with them during their visit.

Consider the person you have in the role of collecting payments. They must be brave—it's not easy to ask people for money. The team member handling your accounts receivable should be incredibly organized and detail-oriented. They need the skills to make tough phone calls and navigate difficult conversations. And remember, these conversations don't have to be unpleasant. They should be conducted with empathy and compassion. You can maintain a kind tone of voice and use verbiage that positions you as an advocate for the patient, helping them handle their financial obligations. This transforms the dynamic and makes the entire process smoother.

Best Practices for Sending Statements

If a past-due balance was not successfully collected at the time of service, you can move on to sending statements. Different dental software offers various types of reports, but the key ones to focus on are those showing patients with an outstanding balance with no open claim. This represents an accurate balance due.

Before communicating with the patient, perform mini chart audits. These confirm that insurance was applied correctly, adjustments were appropriately made, and that the balance reflected is indeed what the patient owes. This way, you can avoid requesting a payment that isn't due. Also, be sure to manage the messages on the statements. Many software systems allow you to add custom messages, so constantly review these messages to verify they are still

LINDA KANE

applicable. For instance, you might have added a specific message last month that no longer applies this month. If not updated, this could lead to confusion and errors. Always pull up the list, check that the right message is there, and then send. This attention to detail prevents mix-ups and maintains clarity and professionalism in your billing process.

I strongly recommend sending statements every week. This breaks down the task into manageable chunks and creates an environment for continuous cash flow to your office. A structured approach works best. For instance, you can organize the sending schedule by the patients' last names: Week one for last names starting with A to D, week two for E to L, week three for M to R, and lastly, week four for S to Z. This method provides a balanced monthly distribution and allows the process to be less overwhelming and more systematic.

To enhance this process further, use the technical tools available through your software. Before sending the statements, I always print an audit trail of the patients I'll address that week. I audit each account for accuracy—reviewing the last statement, the last payment, previous communications, and any messages added to the statement.

Consider integrating modern communication methods like texting. For smaller balances, such as those $30 and under, sending a text with a payment link is often more effective. This direct approach can expedite payments without needing a formal statement, and patients usually respond positively to this convenience.

Staying on Top of Outstanding Balances

Managing outstanding balances is key to maintaining a healthy cash flow in your practice. I advise regularly monitoring reports highlighting accounts with balances with no open claims. This should be a joint effort between the accounts receivable personnel and the doctor. The doctor can provide insights into whether certain patients are family members, neighbors, or friends and how they prefer those accounts handled. The doctor's authorization will also be necessary when sending a patient to collections, especially after all collection attempts have been exhausted.

However, remember that this system, while necessary, shouldn't become your primary focus. Ideally, if you conduct financial consults effectively, collect payments at the time of service, or set up recurring payments, you won't find yourself in situations where you have to send numerous statements or chase people down. Aim to make your operations proactive rather than reactive. Establishing sound financial practices right from the patient's first visit makes everyone's lives easier.

Modernizing Payment Methods

I've seen tremendous success with dental practices that have leveraged technology to streamline billing and collections. Many systems integrate seamlessly with your software to enhance efficiency and ease in collecting outstanding funds.

One effective strategy is text-to-pay or email payments. These methods allow patients to click on a link directly from their phone or email to pay their bills instantly. In the past, you might have relied solely on a "Pay Now" button on your website, and while that still works, using text messages linked to a payment portal offers a more direct and accessible option for most patients. We live on our phones, so capitalizing on that fact can significantly improve payment timeliness.

Here's how it typically works: send mass texts or emails with an embedded payment link—the software tracks who opens these messages. After a week, send a follow-up text to those who opened the message but didn't pay. For example, "Hi Jane, we noticed you haven't settled your balance due from [date]. Could we assist you in completing this payment?" If the message wasn't opened, it might indicate the patient isn't tech-savvy, prompting the need to print and mail a statement instead.

Additionally, consider utilizing innovative software systems, like iCore, which facilitate payments similar to consumer-friendly apps like Venmo, Google Pay, or Samsung Pay. These systems often have a simple tablet interface, making them easy and familiar for patients to use.

Each interaction—whether a text, an email, or a mailed statement—should be meticulously recorded in the patient's chart to ensure clarity and continuity in your billing process.

The Impact of Automation on Billing Efficiency

Automation has significantly improved billing processes in dental offices, particularly those struggling with accounts receivable issues. Let me share an example from my recent experience with two offices facing major AR challenges.

Both offices had transitioned to using powerful software called Open Dental. However, Open Dental alone doesn't handle sending statements; integration with a third-party system is required for that functionality. Each office chose a different system to partner with, but the outcomes were quite similar.

Initially, these offices lacked effective collection systems at their front ends, which led to many outstanding balances. To tackle this, we implemented a strategy involving mass text and email communications to patients with confirmed balances. The response was immediate and positive—payments started coming in as the text-to-pay options were utilized. However, not all third-party systems are alike. One had a much more streamlined approach, whereas the other was more hands-on. So look into ease and functionality, not just cost!

Both of these offices are now actively learning how to set up their financial interactions correctly right from the start, realizing that having to chase payments down is anything but fun. Though they were two very different offices with different circumstances, they learned that every problem has a solution. Most of the time, it's just a matter of learning to do things better. And it's always amazing to see the resulting transformation.

Striving for Continual Improvement and Solutions

The topic of cybersecurity is becoming increasingly hot, especially in a world where threats are growing more sophisticated. A cybersecurity breach in 2024 that impacted Change Healthcare—a major processor of dental and medical claims—reminded us of our vulnerabilities. This incident had a ripple effect across numerous dental offices, disrupting the ability to send claims and patient statements.

During this crisis, our team, along with the broader dental community, faced many challenges. Dental Facebook groups became forums for office managers to voice their frustrations and seek solutions. Thankfully, companies like Patterson Eaglesoft, which relied on Change Healthcare, responded swiftly. They partnered with Vyne Trellis, a platform unaffected by the breach, to resume sending claims, although this solution didn't address the entire problem.

Other industry giants like Dental Intelligence, Flex, and iCore Connect stepped in, offering integrated solutions that solved the immediate issues and propelled practices towards more advanced technological solutions. This was a forced leap into newer technologies, but it placed dental practices in a much better position than before, enabling them to process claims and communicate with patients more efficiently.

From this experience, we learned the importance of safeguarding against such risks. My company, Zeroed-In Dental Solutions, employs several stringent security measures:

- We use Virtual Private Networks (VPNs) and Splashtop to connect to doctors' computers securely.
- We avoid using personal devices for any client-related activities.
- We never have access to your systems as administrators, so we ask that you permit us to do only what is within our scope of work.
- All team members must have a liability policy that includes errors and omissions with cybersecurity endorsements.

Efficiency, security, and proactive management are vital to maintaining the financial operations of a dental office, from billing systems and patient communication strategies to embracing technology and cybersecurity measures. Even in the face of disruptions like cybersecurity breaches, the dental community's resilience and innovative spirit have paved the way for better, more secure systems. Dentistry is a remarkable field, consisting of brilliant minds and the continual drive to improve. Always embrace the opportunities to enhance your practice to stand up to the challenges of an ever-changing world while staying financially healthy.

KEY TAKEAWAYS

⮑ Streamline collections by enforcing payment at the time of service and using automated payment systems like text-to-pay to improve efficiency and patient satisfaction.

⮑ Audit accounts and statements regularly to ensure accuracy and professionalism in communication. This reduces errors and enhances trust in the billing process.

⮑ Adopt a structured weekly billing schedule, utilizing dental software tools for systematic processing and tracking of patient accounts, making the task more manageable.

⮑ Implement security measures to protect sensitive information and prepare for potential cybersecurity threats, ensuring compliance and safeguarding the practice's reputation.

⮑ Continuously explore and integrate new technologies to keep the practice's operations efficient, such as leveraging innovative billing software and enhancing patient communication strategies.

LINDA KANE

CHAPTER NINE

NAVIGATING INSURANCE
WITH CONFIDENCE

I n the dental business, handling insurance matters is a complex role requiring high skill and training. It's not something that can be quickly taught or mastered overnight. It involves navigating a maze of rules and regulations, understanding Explanations of Benefits (EOBs), spotting downgrades, and recognizing contractual laws. The team member managing your claims must be well-versed in these areas and possess years of experience dealing with the intricacies that come with them. Without this expertise, dental practices risk financial losses and exposure to fraud.

Dentists are exceptionally trained to handle the clinical aspects of dentistry, mastering procedures inside the mouth. Yet, many dentists graduate from dental school with little to no knowledge of how to run the business side of their practice, particularly in managing insurance. This education gap often leaves them unaware of what's happening with their insurance processes, focusing instead on clinical outputs like collections, production, and the frustrations of insurance write-offs.

One of the most significant challenges dental offices face with insurance is the lack of adequate systems to manage it. Proper management should involve systematic steps like regularly pulling and reviewing outstanding claims reports—categorized by age (90+, 60+, and 30+ days) and ensuring all insurance funds are posted before these reports are generated. Unfortunately, many offices fail to follow up on these reports, leading to unaddressed claims.

Another common issue is dealing with rejected claims. Offices must check these rejections thoroughly, correct them, and resubmit promptly, which varies in difficulty depending on the clearinghouse used.

An often neglected aspect of insurance management is appealing denials. Offices frequently adjust off unpaid treatments instead of appealing them, potentially forgoing rightful payments. These oversights highlight why having a highly trained professional manage your claims is so important. The knowledge and systems they bring to the table can help safeguard your practice's financial health.

Essential Skills and Training for Managing Dental Insurance Claims

To effectively manage claims, a coordinator must understand insurance laws, compliance standards, and the intricacies of contractual adjustments specific to each office's signed insurance contracts. They must also be able to interpret a wide array of Explanations of Benefits (EOBs), identify critical information for appeals, and communicate policy details to patients. Essentially, they need to be highly trained insurance gurus.

Given the specialized knowledge required, dental offices often decide to train their team internally or outsource these functions. Outsourcing can be strategic, allowing the dental team to focus primarily on patient care rather than getting bogged down by insurance complexities. Hiring an external insurance expert can also be more cost-effective than employing an onsite specialist.

Factors to Consider When Outsourcing Insurance Billing

Whether to outsource insurance billing is a major decision for any dental practice. To assist in this decision, I've compiled a top 10 list of reasons why you might consider outsourcing:

1. **Staffing Issues:** Frequent turnover or difficulty in hiring skilled team members
2. **Undertrained Team:** Lack of expertise in handling complex billing issues
3. **Accounts Receivable Problems:** Collections are lower than they should be
4. **Overloaded Front Office:** The front office team is head down in insurance vs. focusing on patient care.
5. **Increase in Unscheduled Treatments:** Case acceptance percentages are low, and chairs are not as full as they should be
6. **Lagging Recall Systems:** Inefficient patient recall affecting regular visits
7. **Delayed Payments:** Longer wait times for insurance claims to be paid

8. **Rise in Rejected Claims:** An increase in the number of claims rejected by insurance companies
9. **Credentialing Issues:** Challenges associated with new doctors in the practice
10. **Suboptimal Revenue:** The practice is not maximizing possible earnings

A Note about Staffing Issues

Staffing shortages have significantly impacted dental offices since the COVID-19 pandemic hit in 2020, causing employment challenges in the dental field. Many practices nationwide struggle to find hygienists, dental assistants, and exceptionally trained front office employees. Training someone to manage insurance in a dental office is not only lengthy but also heavily depends on the trainer's own knowledge and expertise. If the trainer has only minimal understanding, the quality of training provided can be suboptimal.

Given these challenges, many long-practicing dentists, especially those with 20 or more years of experience, may find themselves working within a constrained framework, or "box," that limits their operational flexibility. This can lead to inefficiencies such as high no-show rates, lower collections, and excessive write-offs. In this context, outsourcing insurance management emerges as a viable strategy.

However, outsourcing has its own set of considerations. I recommend conducting thorough research before choosing an outsourcing partner. Does the billing company adhere strictly to HIPAA regulations to protect information? Do they access the practice's system with appropriate permissions and not as administrators? Are they based in the USA and have relevant experience in a dental office setting? Are they using a secure connection like a Virtual Private Network (VPN) to interact with your office software?

These considerations are critical in ensuring that the outsourcing of insurance functions alleviates staffing shortages and enhances the operational efficiency and security of your dental practice. By carefully selecting a qualified and trustworthy insurance billing partner, you can maintain high standards of insurance management despite reduced in-house resources.

The Benefits of Outsourcing

Once you have decided to outsource insurance billing, there are several benefits to enjoy:

- **Consistent Cash Flow and a Happier Team:** Faster reimbursements and decreased errors lead to better financial stability
- **Patient-Focused Dental Team:** Frees up team members to focus on patient interaction and care, enhancing patient satisfaction and loyalty
- **Maximum Reimbursement:** Expertise in coding and staying on top of changes ensures that the practice receives what it is entitled to
- **Cost Savings on Staffing:** Outsourcing can be more economical than hiring full-time team members, considering salaries and benefits
- **Efficiency and Profitability:** Outsourcing experts can provide insights and improvements to practice workflows
- **Safety and Compliance:** Ensures adherence to legal standards and protects against fraud and embezzlement

Consider that an average dental office insurance coordinator makes $22.00/hour. This will cost you between $45,760 and $64,064, depending on the annual benefits you offer, such as paid time off, insurance benefits, 401K contributions, bonuses, etc., and expenses like unemployment insurance.

Zeroed-In's fees are based on a percentage of your insurance collections. For example, if you collect $45,000 in insurance collections, your Zeroed-In fee is $1,575.00/month (a yearly cost of $18,900.00). If we take the low end of the salary at $45,760 minus $18,900, you save $26,860 by outsourcing your dental insurance billing!

For offices that prefer to develop in-house expertise, one effective strategy is to have an existing skilled insurance coordinator create a comprehensive training manual. This manual should include copies of various EOBs, coding examples, verbiage, and detailed guidelines on posting insurance payments. Developing this resource requires time and diligence but is an invaluable tool for training new coordinators.

Alternatively, dental practices can engage professional services to train their teams. The Zeroed-In team helps protect offices from fraud and embezzlement. We employ only people who reside in the United States and follow guidelines from the American Dental Association and compliance investigators. We care deeply about educating the offices we work with to do things in compliance with the contracts and rules. Just as doctors follow OSHA standards to keep the clinical team safe, we follow compliance standards to protect dental businesses.

Timing is Everything

Insurance companies are actively adjusting their policies and operations, significantly impacting dental practices. These changes are part of a broader strategy involving financial control and operational efficiency. For example, a notable shift has occurred with third-party processors: Availity, previously handling claims and verifying benefits for insurers like Anthem, has been replaced by United Concordia. MetLife recently tightened its timely filing requirements to 30 days as of January 2024. While MetLife processes claims swiftly, this poses a problem when dealing with secondary insurances that may not be as prompt, potentially leading to payment delays. Similarly, Regence has reduced its timely filing window to 90 days and enforces this rule stringently. Another significant change from Blue Cross involved updating all their ID numbers, posing a challenge for practices that do not consistently collect new insurance cards or fail to update these details in their systems.

These changes can disrupt internal claims processing, leading to delays and increased outstanding claims. For practices to manage these complexities, it's crucial to have someone deeply familiar with the current insurance climate. This individual must proactively monitor changes, understand their implications, and adapt processes accordingly.

Verifying Benefits Before Patient Visits

Part of meeting timing requirements is ensuring patient benefits are consistently verified. This creates a more positive overall patient experience and helps avoid claims processing delays. I recommend a few key processes for effective insurance verification:

- **Obtain and Scan Insurance Cards:** The front desk team should obtain a copy of the patient's insurance card upon each visit and scan it into the practice's document center or imaging system. This step ensures that the most current insurance information is readily available.

- **Use Third-Party Verification Portals:** Tools like Icore Verify, Dental Intel's Verifications via Vyne, or similar platforms should be utilized to streamline the verification process. These portals provide quick access to detailed benefit information, reducing the need for lengthy phone calls.

- **Direct Communication with Insurance Providers:** In cases where digital tools do not suffice, or specific queries need to be addressed, calling the insurance company is still necessary. This step helps confirm the details of a patient's coverage and understand any unique policy stipulations.

Verification of insurance benefits should be conducted at a minimum one day ahead of the patient's appointment. However, a more proactive approach involves verifying benefits at least a week beforehand. This timeframe allows the practice to address policy terminations and contact the patient for updated information if necessary. I encourage the insurance coordinator to verify benefits for all hygiene patients and any other patients who have not had their insurance verified within the last three months. A quick check to confirm the policy remains active for patients with previously verified policies is sufficient.

Proactive verification ensures that the practice can provide patients with accurate treatment estimates based on their current benefits, significantly enhancing patient trust and satisfaction. Not to mention, submitting a "clean" claim, complete with all required information, facilitates faster processing and payment by the insurance company. "Unclean" claims, which may have outdated or incorrect information, will likely be rejected, necessitating additional time and resources to resolve.

Creating Positive Change

Our journey with a dental office in Wyoming illustrates the impact of efficient insurance management. This practice faced significant challenges in retaining trained employees, a common issue in areas with limited access to specialized workforce. When the long-standing office manager relocated, the practice struggled to manage patient appointments and financial collections.

My team stepped in and provided comprehensive support, including insurance verifications, billing, and utilizing Dentrix software—all at less than half the cost of hiring an additional employee. The doctor expressed her relief and satisfaction, noting that our services allowed her practice to survive and thrive by focusing on patient relationships rather than administrative burdens. Michelle, a Dentrix expert from our team, became an integral part of their operations, ensuring that the practice could grow even in challenging staffing conditions.

Another story comes from a big university town, where dental practices typically employ university students or their spouses. This demographic shift results in a high turnover rate, with team members staying, on average, only one to four years. The particular practice we helped faced this exact challenge, constantly having to hire new team members, which disrupted the continuity and efficiency of the practice.

Upon engaging with our team, the doctor found that our dedicated efforts improved their office operations. Our commitment to their success transformed how they managed their practice, ultimately reshaping the doctor's views on running a dental business. The feedback was overwhelmingly positive, with the doctor praising our team for making the business more successful and for the personal care shown towards their needs.

We've seen firsthand the transformations that occur when practices decide to tackle their challenges by seeking external expertise. Remember that the journey to improving your practice is continuous and often requires making bold decisions. Whether through internal adjustments or partnering with specialized services, each step you take is towards a more efficient and patient-centered practice.

KEY TAKEAWAYS

- Understanding and managing dental insurance requires specific skills and extensive training in regulations and contractual laws to avoid financial loss.

- Many dentists lack the necessary business acumen, particularly in insurance management, which can significantly impact their practice's financial health.

- Implementing systematic insurance management processes, such as regular reviews of outstanding claims and thorough follow-ups, is critical for maintaining financial stability.

- Outsourcing insurance billing can be strategic and cost-effective. It allows dental offices to focus on patient care while ensuring efficient handling of insurance matters.

- Continuous education and adaptation to insurance policy and procedure changes are essential for maximizing reimbursements and maintaining operational efficiency.

LINDA KANE

CHAPTER TEN

MAXIMIZING PRACTICE REVENUE

Change is inevitable in any dental office, and you must embrace it for ongoing success. It's a reality I've observed countless times: outstanding systems and team members might be in place one day, and the next, you're facing turnover. Imagine you have a top-notch dental biller who suddenly retires or a team member you've invested heavily in training decides to part ways due to various life events. These scenarios are almost guaranteed over the lifespan of your practice. When these changes occur, it's not just about filling a position; it's about maintaining the standard of care and operational efficiency your practice is known for. Investing in your team's ongoing education and robust systems ensures they can adapt without compromising quality. Every new team member needs training and integration into your practice's culture and workflows. In the dental game of life, being proactive about these changes keeps a practice at the top of the leaderboard.

Strategies for Revenue Growth Without Compromising Care

Let's break down the six essential systems every dental practice should focus on to not only boost revenue but also enhance patient satisfaction and retention:

1. Optimizing the New Patient Experience

The journey begins with a prospective patient's first interaction with your practice. An outstanding new patient experience converts inquiries into loyal patients. This system sets the tone for the relationship and can influence a patient's decision to choose you.

2. Managing the Recall Program

Once patients are in your system, you must keep them engaged and returning for regular visits. A recall program ensures that patients do not slip through the cracks and receive timely reminders for follow-up care, keeping your practice's schedule full and consistent. A dedicated team member should be responsible for managing the recall system. Hygienists, given their direct relationship with patients, are ideally positioned to schedule the next appointment while the patient is still in the chair. This proactive approach saves time and significantly increases the likelihood that patients will return.

Monitoring the percentage of patients reappointed by hygienists is essential to evaluate the effectiveness of your recall strategy. This metric highlights the importance of this responsibility and provides clear performance data. Addressing any miscommunication is also key; for example, ensuring that hygienists and the front desk are clear on scheduling follow-ups can prevent oversights and improve patient booking rates.

Advanced software allows practices to pull detailed reports on pre-scheduling metrics. For patients who choose not to schedule immediately, employing third-party software to automate follow-ups can be incredibly powerful. These follow-ups should be scheduled regularly and utilize several communication methods such as texts, emails, phone calls, and postcards to cater to patient preferences.

3. Maximizing Unscheduled Treatment and Case Acceptance

A common misconception among dental professionals is that treatment consultations and case acceptance are the same. However, a treatment consultation discusses costs, while case acceptance occurs when a patient commits to proceeding with the recommended treatment. Streamlining these processes can significantly impact your practice's bottom line.

An effective tactic is to ensure that every patient leaves the office with a scheduled next visit (NV) or a clear reason for return (RFR), as noted in their clinical records. This information should be communicated seamlessly to the front office during the patient's checkout, emphasizing the importance of booking their next appointment, whether for treatment or a routine hygiene visit.

Despite best efforts, there will inevitably be treatments that remain unscheduled. Traditional methods like printing reports of unscheduled treatments and manually adding notes are time-consuming and often not actionable. Instead, modern software solutions enable direct communication with patients about their pending treatments at the click of a button, even sending mass messages to patients who meet specific criteria. Let's say that you have a last-minute opening for a two-hour slot on a Tuesday afternoon. With the right software, you can quickly identify patients who prefer appointments on Tuesdays, have unused insurance benefits, and require a procedure like a crown. A simple search and text message can fill that slot almost instantly. This optimizes the doctor's schedule and helps patients utilize their available benefits before they expire.

4. Skilled Insurance and Billing Management

A competent individual who can handle insurance claims and billing is crucial. The key to success in this area is accuracy and proactivity. The first step is to ensure that you gather all necessary patient information before they even step into the office. This includes verifying benefits to prevent any miscommunication about coverage, which can lead to incorrect billing and uncomfortable conversations with patients.

Strive to create claims with meticulous attention to detail—incorporating the correct notes, codes, and fees and sending them to the right insurance company with the correct member ID. Operating with a proactive mindset streamlines the billing process and prevents delays and complications that can arise from errors. These delays often result in increased costs as the team spends more time in reactive mode, addressing issues that could have been avoided.

Another strategy to consider is outsourcing your insurance billing. This can be more cost-effective not only in financial terms but also in terms of compliance and efficiency. Outsourcing to specialists can safeguard your practice from compliance issues, often resulting in more treatments being appealed rather than written off. This means that practices usually collect more revenue than they would if managed internally. Experts can help you receive quicker, more accurate payments and reduce the administrative burden on your team. This allows your team to focus more on patient care and less on the complexities of insurance processing, making it a smart choice for many dental offices aiming to optimize their operations and boost their bottom line.

5. Regular Statements and Accounts Management

Sending out regular billing statements and actively managing accounts receivable are key to maintaining healthy cash flow. It's important to keep past-due numbers low and collections high by having dedicated team members managing this system.

6. Aligning Insurance Fees for Optimal Reimbursemen

Navigating the complexities of fee management based on demographic studies and insurance negotiations is crucial for maintaining the financial health of dental practices. Unfortunately, the days when individual practice owners could directly negotiate their insurance fee schedules with insurance companies are behind us. For example, Delta Dental, a national insurance provider, and other companies now have set schedules for releasing updated fee schedules—some annually and others at various times throughout the year.

Understanding where your practice stands regarding competitive pricing can be enhanced by utilizing the resources offered by sales teams who visit dental offices. These teams often provide a free study of your demographic's top 40 dental codes. This analysis helps practices determine if their fees are aligned with the desired percentile—most aiming to be in the 80th percentile.

Many practices find themselves entangled in what I call a

"spaghetti bowl" of insurance fee schedules if they have been under contract with insurance providers for many years. To untangle and organize these schedules, I recommend working with specialists like the team at Profitable PPOs out of Arizona. Led by Clint, they excel in meticulously analyzing each contract. They create detailed spreadsheets comparing your practice's fees against multiple insurance fee schedules, identifying whether these schedules are proprietary or leased from other companies. Their approach is not just about simplification but also about optimization. They advocate for dental practices to align contracts most beneficially, often beyond the top 40 codes, providing a comprehensive view of where to position your fee schedule. The outcomes can be transformative—instead of substantial write-offs on procedures like crowns, which could range from $300 to $600, adjustments are reduced to less than $100. This strategic alignment allows practices to minimize losses from high insurance write-offs and, in turn, significantly boost their revenue.

For example, I encountered a dental practice heavily involved with various PPOs in Boise, Idaho. Over the years, they were entangled in numerous insurance contracts set up by previous managers and team members, creating a complex maze of commitments that perfectly illustrated the "spaghetti bowl." This situation presented a significant challenge but also a unique opportunity for transformation.

The practice was contracted with nearly every major insurance provider, and deciphering these contracts to understand their impact on the practice's finances was daunting. To address this, we conducted a thorough analysis, pulling extensive patient lists to understand which patients were covered under which plans and assessing the potential impacts of any changes we might consider. Recognizing the need for expert assistance, I recommended partnering with Profitable PPOs, having worked with the owner's father, a dentist, for over a decade. Their reputation for integrity and excellence gave us confidence in taking bold steps forward.

Their initial phase involved creating detailed spreadsheets that laid out our current fee schedules and what we were contracted for with each insurance. Clint, from Profitable PPOs, was instrumental in this phase. He met with us to review these documents and outlined two potential paths we could take. We decided to consolidate most of our contracts under the Careington umbrella, which covered insurers like MetLife, Cigna, Aetna, and others. This strategic move significantly improved our fee schedules—astonishingly, we adjusted only $15 on a crown, a dramatic reduction from the usual several hundred dollars.

However, we couldn't apply these changes to our local Delta Dental contracts due to their non-negotiable terms, but the improvements in all other areas were substantial. The fee restructuring process was a financial investment and a time-consuming one, spanning about 13 months. Yet, the outcome was overwhelmingly positive, making it a worthwhile endeavor for practices looking to optimize their financial operations.

By focusing on these six systems, your practice can unearth a goldmine of opportunities that do not require additional physical labor from the doctor, such as doing more implants or crowns. Instead, it's about leveraging what's already within your practice to its fullest potential.

Finding Light in the Shadows

"Working smarter, not harder" is a mantra often repeated across various professions, but it resonates much more profoundly in dentistry. Throughout my career, I've been driven by a passion to help practice owners succeed and thrive. Dentists endure years of rigorous training and substantial financial investments to establish their practices. Beyond the technical challenges, they manage facilities, equipment, and teams—a relentless task that can become overwhelmingly stressful without the proper support.

The emotional toll of dentistry is not often discussed but is deeply felt within the community. It's a profession with a hidden side, marked by significant stress and, unfortunately, a higher incidence of depression. This reality hit home in the most heart-wrenching way in my last position, where I worked with a doctor who was a colleague and a dear friend. He was a remarkable person who impacted everyone around him. Tragically, the overwhelming pressures led him to take his own life. Experiencing this loss was the hardest thing I've ever faced professionally and a stark reminder of the critical need for support within our profession.

This experience reinforced my commitment to providing relief and guidance for dentists. The systems I advocate for are ones I've implemented myself and seen transform practices from the inside out. I don't teach theoretical models; I share practical, tested strategies that reduce stress and increase efficiency. When I teach teams how to manage effective systems step by step, I help them understand that working smarter, not harder, is possible.

Implementing the right systems and training your team to manage them can alleviate the daily pressures of running a dental practice. It's about focusing on what truly matters, streamlining processes, and ensuring everyone is aligned and working cohesively. Magic happens when a practice zeroes in on the right things; it transforms the work environment into positivity and focused energy.

As we close this chapter and this book, I hope the stories and strategies shared here inspire you to look at your practice not as a burden that might overpower you but as a space filled with potential for joy and success. Remember, the light at the end of the tunnel isn't an oncoming train. It's the bright future illuminated by the changes you implement to make your professional life manageable and truly rewarding. Let's zero in on making your dental practice the magical place it can be, one step at a time.

KEY TAKEAWAYS

➲ Embrace change and maintain high standards by investing in team education and solid systems, crucial for managing transitions like turnover or retirement.

➲ Enhance patient satisfaction and retention by optimizing the new patient experience and managing recall programs effectively.

➲ Invest in skilled insurance and billing management to streamline processes, reduce errors, and ensure timely reimbursements, considering outsourcing to reduce administrative burdens and improve efficiency.

➲ Assess and align insurance fee schedules regularly to optimize reimbursement rates and maintain financial health, utilizing expert consultants if necessary to navigate complex insurance contracts.

➲ Implement and continuously refine systems and training for your team to alleviate daily operational pressures. Focusing on strategic management creates a supportive work environment that helps prevent burnout and the overwhelming stress that can be present in the dental profession.

EPILOGUE

*"You don't have to be great to start, but
you do have to start to be great!"*
-Zig Ziglar

Thank you for taking the time to read this book—a true labor of love for me. You've embarked on a significant journey by arming yourself with the strategies necessary to transform your dental practice. It's not as difficult as it may seem; it simply requires the willingness to acknowledge a problem and then take decisive action to fix it. Having learned from some of the best minds in the industry, I felt compelled to share this knowledge with you. I hope this book has inspired you to view your practice through a wide-angle lens and explore the exciting possibilities that await.

Now that you've turned the last page, you are equipped to see beyond the confines of the proverbial box. This book is your tool to foster positive change, whether in your leadership style or understanding the dynamics of your front office. Are they simply reacting to daily demands, or are they proactively working to cultivate your office culture and enhance patient care? It's time to evaluate every aspect of your practice, from insurance policies to patient recall programs. Perhaps now is the moment to consider outsourcing your insurance handling to a reputable company—a potential game changer for your office.

Remember, the power to choose is entirely yours. What you've learned here is grounded in proven practices that have transformed dental offices from the brink of bankruptcy to thriving enterprises. If you ignore this new knowledge, you risk continuing in the same unproductive patterns. How healthy are your insurance claims? What about your recall program? How much unscheduled treatment is going unnoticed? Address these questions now. Every dental office faces these issues, but the real change comes from tackling them head-on.

So, what's the next step? Let's start with a complimentary discovery session. Go to my calendar link at **zeroedinbook.com** to book a 15-30-minute consultation so I can learn about you and your practice and address any questions or concerns. This is your opportunity to take the first steps toward improvement.

From here, we can prioritize the most impactful changes. What awaits you is a more precise alignment with your team, ensuring you have the right people in place and creating an improved office culture focused more on patient care than paperwork. I specialize in optimizing your staff's roles and managing your insurance efficiently through my team of specialists, turning what was once a burden into a profitable aspect of your practice. None of this is possible without your leadership. I am here to coach you through this transformative process, helping you create not just a functioning office but a magical environment where everyone thrives.

Let's zero in on making your practice the magical place it can be, one step at a time. Schedule your complimentary Zeroed-In session at:

RescueMyDentalOffice.com

ABOUT THE AUTHOR

LINDA KANE
FOUNDER
ZEROED-IN DENTAL SOLUTIONS

Linda Kane, Founder of Zeroed-In Dental Solutions, began her career in dentistry in 1999 at a solo practice in Greeley, Colorado. She's worn every hat in the business office throughout her career and managed solo and group practices. On her journey, she became a seasoned billing specialist and industry consultant. Linda's passion for dentistry has remained unwavering.

With a wealth of experience and her commitment to staying modern and efficient, Linda is not your average coach. She deeply understands every aspect of dental office operations, and she leads a team of specialists who share her devotion to care for their practices and promote their revenue optimization.

When faced with the challenges of 2020, Linda observed dental

offices struggling to retain their teams. Armed with home-baked cookies and flyers, she began visiting offices across Idaho to personally introduce herself and Zeroed-In's unique approach to supporting dental practices. Zeroed-In Dental Solutions has significantly impacted numerous offices, backed by glowing reviews from satisfied clients.

But Linda's not all business—she's also a proud single mom of two amazing kids and one beautiful grandson! She's a dog mom to two adorable Aussiedoodle rescues. In her downtime, she enjoys baking and watching her favorite TV shows.

Linda Kane and Zeroed-In Dental Solutions embody integrity, community, and empowerment in modern dentistry. Under her leadership, Zeroed-In Dental Solutions is committed to equipping every dental team with the tools it needs to thrive.

WHAT LINDA'S CLIENTS ARE SAYING...

"To any Office Manager or office staff who is overworked and overwhelmed trying to keep up with the claims race, this company is for you! They are friendly and helpful, and they know their stuff! So wishing we would have hired Zeroed-In sooner! It's so nice to know claims are being consistently sent and paid! They offer help in all areas: claims, statements, insurance verification, etc. Best stress reducer ever! Worth every penny! Highly recommend them!"

- Dr. Ryan. Smith, The Dental Health Center, Rexburg, ID

—

"If there were such a reality show as Dental Office Rescue, Linda would be the host! I am a new practice owner and was just getting ready to close on a practice that was having some significant challenges. The billing and insurance filing was an absolute disaster, and most of the staff had quit before I could even take over. I relayed all of this to Linda, and she knew what I needed to succeed before I could even grasp the loftiness of the challenge, my dental knight in shining armor!

Linda flew out and spent a week in my office, training a brand-new team on brand-new software with a brand-new positive and fun culture. I should mention that this new team had never worked in the dental space. Not only did she help unravel some of the disorganization of the mess I inherited, but she also set me up for success beyond my wildest expectations. It was almost effortless getting her billing specialists set up to take care of the insurance claims, and they have done an incredible job working with my team to make the process seamless.

She left us that week with an energized and enthusiastic team, ready to take on the challenges of running this exciting new dental practice. What makes Linda special, though, is not her genius of the front office or organization with billing systems; it is her pure joy and compassion that permeates every room she walks in. She filled my fledgling office with a light and positivity that I desperately needed and for which I am forever grateful."

- Dr. Alexandra Arnold, Vail Dental Design, Vail, CO

—

"BEST money spent! What Zeroed-In offers is a wealth of knowledge and extremely valuable experience from an expert team. The amount of stress that Zeroed-In takes off our shoulders makes owning our own business a little bit more manageable. Tough to find this quality of service nowadays. Highly recommend them!"

- Dr. Jed Zirker, Zirker Family Dentistry, Ammon, ID

—

"Linda, you are one of the best teachers I have ever observed, and I've had some great ones. You are non-threatening; you gauge your audience well and know how much information to teach at one time. You have a wonderful spirit about you with complete harmony with heart and mind. Thanks for your example."

- Dr. Eric Ballou, Lake Harbor Dental & Garden Valley Smiles, Boise, Garden Valley, ID

—